THE
CLUTTER
REMEDY

THE
CLUTTER
REMEDY

A Guide to Getting Organized for Those Who Love Their Stuff

MARLA STONE

New World Library
Novato, California

New World Library
14 Pamaron Way
Novato, California 94949

Text design by Tona Pearce Myers

Library of Congress Cataloging-in-Publication Data
Names: Stone, Marla, date, author.
Title: The clutter remedy : a guide to getting organized for those who love their stuff / Marla Stone.
Description: Novato, California : New World Library, [2019] | Summary: "A former therapist turned professional organizer helps readers eliminate clutter in their homes and offices. Instead of merely encouraging readers to throw away their possessions, the author shows them how to make their personal spaces harmonious with their values, personalities, and lifestyles."-- Provided by publisher.
Identifiers: LCCN 2019035895 (print) | LCCN 2019035896 (ebook) | ISBN 9781608686292 (paperback) | ISBN 9781608686308 (epub)
Subjects: LCSH: Storage in the home. | House cleaning. | Orderliness.
Classification: LCC TX309 .S74 2019 (print) | LCC TX309 (ebook) | DDC 648/.5--dc23
LC record available at https://lccn.loc.gov/2019035895
LC ebook record available at https://lccn.loc.gov/2019035896

First printing, December 2019
ISBN 978-1-60868-629-2
Ebook ISBN 978-1-60868-630-8
Printed in Canada on 100% postconsumer-waste recycled paper

New World Library is proud to be a Gold Certified Environmentally Responsible Publisher. Publisher certification awarded by Green Press Initiative.

10   9   8   7   6   5   4   3

I would like to dedicate this book to my husband, Brett, and my father, Howard, first and foremost, for all their unwavering and unconditional love and support. This book is also dedicated to all the brave souls who let me into their dwellings, lives, and hearts. I wish you all an organized self and space, for life.

CONTENTS

INTRODUCTION

To live perpetually organized in a clear space using efficient and effective strategies makes your life easier, more relaxing, and productive. If you think getting organized is about getting rid of your stuff, it's not. Instead my Clutter Remedy strategy is inspired by working with people who love their stuff but also feel encumbered by clutter. I see people, worldly goods, and space in a unique way. I don't care how much stuff you own and how much space you have. I don't care what things you keep or discard. It doesn't matter whether you are a millennial, a minimalist, or you have gobs of stuff; what matters is there is a better way to go through your items, admire them, and keep it all rocking your world without upsetting yourself, your space, or your schedule. Instead of wanting to hurl everything out the window or into a dumpster, transforming your life — and space — with stability and confidence is the path to perpetual organized living. My goal is to help you become organized forever, which is accomplished by examining how you view yourself, your life, and your objects.

Reaching the truth about what you value in life is one of the most powerful ways of knowing yourself, your stuff, and your space intimately. By knowing what you truly value in life, you will know how to organize all that you own. Desiring a creative and simplified way to get yourself and your space organized is a normal response to living with clutter. Yet the life you want to lead — full of activity, fun, and purpose — is more important than being a weary and downtrodden clutter caretaker. You want to declutter with grace and dignity — and with a professional flair instead of feeling embarrassed and flustered.

Typically, the fluster and frenzy heighten when you want to find something important before walking out the door, and it's nowhere in sight, making you late and anxious. Or you struggle with an inadequate, failing system of disorganized, ever-growing piles. To stay calm and functioning, day to day, you find yourself hiding your stuff, shoving it in drawers, moving it around, and storing it haphazardly — but you know this is not how to live with the stuff that you love. The round and round "human in a hamster wheel" behavior of going from clutter to clear *and back* to clutter is exhausting. It tires you out and makes you itch for more things to covet, instead of appreciating what you already own.

From my perspective, getting organized is not about cleaning up a closet or a pantry. It's about analyzing the causes and personal challenges associated with cluttered and disorganized environments. Realizing that outer space is a reflection of the inner self helps motivate people to look deeper for the cause of clutter. When a person's mood is off-kilter, it colors how their space will appear. Instead of living in a sacred and splendid space, they will end up living in a cluttered and out-of-control space. A cyclone effect within a home or workspace is often correlated with inner turbulence and commotion. The inner self will also influence how you look at what you own and how you feel about yourself and your appearance.

For instance, an outfit you loved a week ago will suddenly make you feel miserable, but it's not the outfit that is causing your angst. Feelings come from your inner self, processing thoughts and formulating conclusions about your life. When the inner self is cluttered with self-doubt and insecurity, even the most elegant clothing won't inspire feeling confident or beautiful. Your inner state can blind you to the beauty of life and all the things that you love. Since inner, emotional clutter will trigger physical clutter over and over again, it's important to first declutter your emotions and your thoughts. This begins with understanding and articulating what matters to you most. Then and only then will you be able to move forward with the Clutter Remedy strategy. The strategy gives you well-thought-out and specific criteria for all the objects you own, and it helps you become decisive and make good decisions about what to keep in your life. The clutter surrounding you has more meaning than you realize. Matter matters. It has energy, deeper meaning, and charge.

I meet with people regularly who consider their clutter a "secret." Their closest friends are not allowed to see their clutter or are sometimes not even invited into their homes. Some people remark that their excessive clutter or messy space brings on so much "confusion and derailment" that they've stopped enjoying life and feel desperate and isolated. Others share that they are what I call "décor challenged" with blank or overloaded walls, barren or cluttered mantels, and dated or misplaced furniture. However, most admit they have consistent and mild clutter challenges within their closets, drawers, cabinets, and garage, and they want tips for getting and staying organized. Some have overcollected for years

4 THE CLUTTER REMEDY

with no idea what to do with anything, and they are caught up in the mire and muck, believing they are "tied" to it. Others have collected out of boredom and own doubles of everything with no space to store it all.

Ultimately you want to love your stuff and know that everything you own is in your space for a reason. You want to stop having a love/hate relationship with stuff. I know there are days of loving your stuff, your collections, your books, bags, clothes, shoes, jewelry, tchotchkes, and sporting goods, and other days the stuff takes over and becomes an irritant and you want to set it on fire or take an ax to it and bury it in the backyard. Remaining in love with your stuff instead of being at war with it becomes easier when things you own are in alignment with your ideal lifestyle. Then, everything you own will imbue the sparkle and radiance that is part of the inner you. You will shine in your space as much as your space shines back at you in its image of perfection.

Utilizing the creative, simple Clutter Remedy strategy in this guide, I will teach you how to declutter and organize all that you own, now and for the rest of your life. You will become a connoisseur and authority on how to get and stay organized. What does the Clutter Remedy process entail? On a practical level, it takes a commitment of time and some resourcefulness, though how much time depends on the size of your space, on the amount of stuff you own, and on your motivation to fulfill your goals. Yet the process is flexible and can be adapted to any situation and budget. Completing the entire process, from beginning to end, for one large room takes one to three days, while multiple rooms or an entire house could take longer. How fast it takes also depends on your preparation, your energy level, and sometimes the weather.

The Clutter Remedy strategy in itself is simple and easy to use, and once learned, it can be used regularly for effective long-term maintenance. When you make the effort to get organized in this way, it will save you time, money, headaches, and perpetual turmoil. The process teaches you how to live a finely tuned and categorized lifestyle, so that you will have easy access to everything you own, and everything you own will have its ideal placement.

In short, you start with an inner assessment, so that you identify what you truly value in life, then set life goals to achieve the things you are missing, along with clearing and healing any past challenges that are blocking you from getting and staying organized. You'll learn a new way of communicating that will increase your motivation to stay organized, long-term. You then envision and plan your ideal space, and choose the optimal time to get organized. Next, when you start the physical process of getting organized, you arrange your organizing tools and containers, clear your space, categorize everything you own, use the Clear and Concise Criteria to make good decisions about what to keep, fine-tune your categories, and set up your space based on how often and where you use things. As you are quickly clearing your space, you will find things you thought were lost and gone forever — earrings, shoes, old letters, safe deposit keys, and more — and you will be surprised and shocked by laughter and tears.

In one to three days, you will know exactly how many umbrellas, blenders, and books you actually own. You will realize how many shoes, ties, and small electronic items you possess. Living a categorized life means no more "human in a hamster wheel" episodes with your stuff. Getting everything you own categorized and then ultimately fine-tuned is an eye-opening experience. It happens swiftly and efficiently. The adjustment to living clutter-free will be a defining and freeing moment in your life. It will happen with a zest of spirit for wanting order and a final and permanent resting place for everything you own. It will be an uplifting experience that will provide inner clarity and rhythm for keeping your space organized perpetually for the rest of your life.

I became a professional organizer because I love to help

people. I also love to organize, plan, develop space, and decorate. Formerly, I was a social worker and psychotherapist in private practice. After seventeen years of practicing, I ran out of the analyst chair, and what did I do? I ran directly into helping people get organized. I found that I could create new and innovative ways to organize plasticware, paperwork, and any number of things. I had a knack for it and a love for designing spaces. Helping people create better lives for themselves was the icing on the cake. Being a professional organizer is my dream job, so I formed my company I-Deal-Lifestyle Inc., and I developed a highly integrative and precise way of empowering people to achieve their dreams, as well as to manage their stuff and their space independently.

When I first became an organizer, I thought it was only about arranging plasticware and making things neat. What I did not fully appreciate is how much being organized helps heal all aspects of our lives. Lindsay was the first person I helped to get organized. Lindsay was in an unhappy marriage. Her husband was preoccupied. Lindsay had been sleeping on the couch downstairs. She felt alone and shopped to cope with feelings of abandonment. Her house was overwrought with toys and clothes. We filled forty large trash bags with clothes that had taken over her bedroom and closet. She cried in her closet once it was emptied out. At that moment, I realized I was not only there to help Lindsay declutter and redesign her space; I was there to help her reshape her life into prime form. I was there to go into the thick of it with her. I was not there to pick up all the pieces of her life. I was there to pick up all her stuff and help her realize what held meaning for her. I was there to help Lindsay understand what an ideal lifestyle meant to her and to help her dream it up when she didn't know how. I was there to help her make sense about what to keep or toss out of her life, in a way that made sense, rather than in a traumatic or dramatic way. Now, I am here to help you in the same way, with years more experience and so many ideas about how to get you organized for good.

Epiphanies about clutter manifest regularly as people unpack their junk drawers and empty overfilled cabinets and closets. Whether clutter is mild or perpetual or extreme, people experience self-awareness as they process and go through their clutter and mess. When people see the clutter replaced, in a short period of time, by organization and a clear, newly designed space, it takes the sting out of what could be a sensitive, sticky situation. I've discovered that even people who have barricaded themselves in insurmountable mounds of stuff can find insight and the desire and fortitude to get and stay organized for good. All these permanent changes require is taking a considered, deeper look into how you can live a more optimal lifestyle. The exciting thing is that you will learn a new way to make years of clutter disappear, like an abracadabra trick, and without having to get rid of a thing, when that's not in the cards.

After many years of helping thousands of homes and businesses get decluttered, no matter what state they were in, I have honed this precise, easy-to-use strategy to get and stay organized. Creating a long-lasting permanently organized space is by far the best gift to give yourself. Think of it as engaging in a luxury service, but unlike a spa treatment, it will last forever.

Chapter 1 focuses on visualizing and creating your own personal ideal lifestyle and clearing out any emotional challenges that will get in the way of becoming organized. This chapter helps you understand how you became disorganized in the first place, while recognizing your innermost desires and what you value most in life. You will learn strategies to clear and heal old wounds and how to identify your most sacred truth about life. Chapter 2 discusses how changing your language will influence your productivity and keep you motivated to stay perpetually organized long-term. You will learn how the misuse of the word *need*, using indecisive language, and not sharing feelings impact every aspect of your personal and professional life. Understanding actual "needs" — such as air, food, water, shelter, sleep, elimination, and sunlight — is a priority for living a balanced and happier lifestyle. Additionally, putting the word *will* back into your language will change your life. Chapter 3 is the step-by-step Clutter Remedy strategy designed to help you clear your space of clutter, categorize everything you own, and go through everything using my proprietary Clear and Concise Criteria, followed by fine-tuning all your precious belongings and finally setting your space up for success. The Clutter Remedy strategy is designed to turn each and every space into organized and sustainable living and working areas. Learning to live in this unique and settling way is the remedy for clutter. Chapter 4 is centered on organizing room by room and space by space. The step-by-step practices for organizing anything and everything — including your paperwork, garage, kitchen, bathrooms, office, closets, and kids' stuff — will empower you to want to go further and give your space a better design altogether. The process of attaining an organized space is achieved through a simplified and coordinated organizing process, alongside specific considerations for all areas of the home, workplace, and storage areas.

Chapter 5 focuses on how to stay organized throughout the year, helps you identify storage space options for items used infrequently, and discusses common challenges that prevent long-term organization. The suggestions in this chapter will help you stay organized year-round, with clever anecdotes and ideas for being creative with your space through the seasons, holidays, special occasions, and life transitions. Chapter 6 will help you design your space after you have finished decluttering. This chapter will guide you through interior design options and how to set up your space in a way that will keep you organized for good. Setting up your space with all the stuff you love is easy when you see your space with a whole new perspective and add storage options to create an aesthetically pleasing environment, without spending a lot of money. Finally, chapter 7 discusses the most serious challenges and situations that can get in the way of decluttering and becoming organized, such as overcollecting and accumulating, emotional and/or physical challenges, loss and grief, and mental health challenges (like ADD, OCD, OCPD, depression, and hoarding disorder). In these situations, it's absolutely possible to declutter, but professional intervention can be helpful.

Ultimately, working on a better you and creating a better space is a great investment that will enhance all aspects of your life: your health, stability, family, work, and much more. You will be less stressed and experience more happiness by becoming more organized, which is a transferable skill you can use in most situations. You will discover bright and sparkly gems of insight, poignant stories and connections, and useful tools to help you meet any physical, emotional, and mental health challenges, with tips on managing health, well-being, seasons, schedules, family interactions, traveling, moving, and more. I wish you a journey through your clutter to your most organized self and space.

1

ORCHESTRATING YOUR IDEAL, CLUTTER-FREE LIFESTYLE

The process of identifying your core values and an ideal lifestyle — what you truly want to accomplish in life — creates the desire for order, harmony, and a clutter-free residence and work space. The concept of an ideal lifestyle may prove confusing at first because you are so busy putting one foot in front of the other, making decisions throughout the day, and regularly tending to the more mundane aspects of life: work, housekeeping, errands, chauffeuring, cooking, shopping, and everyday tasks. Focusing on your loftiest and forgotten dreams and recognizing your aspirations is the beginning of an emotionally freeing and enlightening journey.

You can experience as much difficulty talking about your innermost secret dreams and desires as you do discussing and revealing your most difficult clutter challenges and the frustrations that go along with staying organized. Having a messy, chaotic, and unpresentable home or workplace can cause deep embarrassment, conflicts, and mixed feelings. When your life goals and desires are not being fulfilled, talking about what you want most out of life can trigger feelings of confusion, regret, and sadness. Becoming open about all that you want is essential to knowing how to live an ideal and clutter-free life.

Some people think they will be able to dig themselves out of their convoluted mess by themselves or with the help of family members. Ironically, fixating on the clutter derails them from focusing on the inner challenges they face: the mess inside of themselves. You are not alone with your clutter challenges. Clutter is an epidemic around the world, and fixing clutter starts by focusing on the inner self.

THE CLUTTER CAMOUFLAGE

Clutter can be mystifying at times, and you will notice that "decluttering" methods are not the cure-all for feeling more optimistic about yourself or better about your life, especially because they rarely last. However, identifying and fulfilling life's larger purpose successfully, and seeing your space and your clutter clearly, will help you maintain an organized space and a clutter-free lifestyle, one that sticks with you for good. What you don't realize is that clutter is simply a camouflage for what you truly want in life. It conceals your dreams and goals. It makes it difficult to see what direction or path to take. Clutter camouflage blows you off course. It can lead to an unintentional and directionless life. You can literally be tripping, not only over your stuff, but over your life purpose as well. In Jeri's case, tripping over books represented avoiding her dreams of being a writer.

For years Jeri had talked about writing poetry, and she had

collected hundreds upon hundreds of poetry books, how-to guides, and an enormous amount of writing apparatuses. When I suggested she could open a small stationery shop, she laughed. Then we discussed the more serious side of things. Jeri had spent a lot of time and money collecting items that she believed would help make her a great writer. From all appearances, the contents of Jeri's small apartment alluded to the idea that she was a fine writer or even a scholar. Yet the more Jeri collected, the less space she had to write. Her desk was unusable, since it was completely covered with books, paper, pens, journals, and highlighters. Jeri's bookshelves were overloaded with books. Books were stacked on the floor and other flat surfaces, the couch, and in her bedroom. Most of her cabinets and drawers were filled to the brim with every possible writing tool imaginable. The more I looked around her space, the clearer the truth became: Jeri's stuff was blocking her from writing and stomping out her dreams of becoming a prolific poet.

Jeri recognized that collecting and owning lots of stuff did not make her more creative. The thing Jeri valued most was self-expression, and she realized her focus was sharing her innermost thoughts about life, not collecting writing tools. By getting her goals straightened out and in clearing up her space, Jeri cleared a spot in her life for writing. She kept most of her stuff, both by utilizing the Clutter Remedy space-planning strategy and by adding a few more bookshelves and cabinets. Jeri kept everything that was useful, everything that served a purpose, sentimental items, and all the things she loved. Jeri's place was whipped into shape, first by broadly categorizing everything she owned, then fine-tuning her items, and finally by finding the perfect containment and home for everything she cherished. Can you relate to Jeri's situation by looking at what you've collected and never used? Is all the stuff you're not using a sign that you are not "using" your inner gifts for loftier goals?

You can go out and buy gadgets, supplies, ingredients, manuals, equipment, electronics, information, and a surplus of products, but if you don't use them, are they a diversion from fulfilling your dreams or a way to fill the emptiness you have inside yourself? Possessions and material objects are not the seeds for growth and development. You know those objects do not define you as a person. You know things don't make situations you desire happen. Obviously, certain things are helpful, once you have the determination and know-how to accomplish your dreams and goals, but *things* don't get you there, *you* do.

STUFF IS JUST STUFF

You know stuff is just stuff. It's inanimate. It is not alive. Personal effects do not have thoughts or feelings, but you may treat them like they do. Possessions can trigger feelings, but they do not create feelings within you. You know you want material objects around, otherwise you wouldn't allow them in your space in the first place. If you didn't love all your wares and worldly goods and you decided to live in an empty room with a minimal amount, I guarantee over time you would start to miss the things you once cherished. But you know the big stuff in life is not stuff. The big stuff in life is loved ones, health, happiness, and living the best life you can.

Living with the basic essentials like a bed, lamps, chairs, a desk, a table, and a couch makes life livable, comfortable, and convenient. Living with shelves, cooking utensils, office supplies, kitchen and bath products, electronics, bedding and towels, toys, and hobby stuff makes life functional, active, and settling. Owning books, trinkets, jewelry, knickknacks, artwork, collections, clothes, and accessories creates an aesthetically pleasing, interesting, and special life. You love stuff for a reason; so there is no reason, at all, to struggle and stress over stuff — ever.

Cluttered environments are not caused by laziness, but rather the lack of a personal, proven strategy. Knowing how to decipher what is important and what is not, by using the Clear and Concise Criteria, prevents clutter from piling up and allows it to be easily processed. The most important thing about conquering clutter, and organizing mounds and pounds of stuff, is having a way to declutter easily, quickly, and efficiently. You don't want to be looking for things you want to use; you want those things quickly and easily. You want your stuff when you want it, in a timely manner, so you will be on time for appointments, events, and meetings. You want things at your fingertips, or at the very least at arm's length, to feel confident and at peace walking out the door or to be spontaneously creative. Your stuff is not supposed to be mysterious — lurking around corners, under the bed, hunted down, or hidden. Your stuff is supposed to be categorized, cherished, and in a special home all of its own.

In cluttered environments, it is near impossible to concentrate on the things that are important to you. The quandary over stuff mostly stems from not knowing and identifying what you value, what to keep, and how to store it all. Solving those three things ends your struggle with stuff immediately. The "tug of war" with stuff starts when things can't be found, when things start to pile up, and when your space becomes full of unruly landmines.

I know you're eager to get decluttered, but before you jump into all of the aerobics involved in space organizing, consider revealing to yourself how you created the clutter in the first place so you will stay organized long-term. Getting decluttered and having your space über-organized is not rocket science, but staying organized for good is. It takes some effort to look into your inner self and to cope with and emit any emotional clutter that is perpetuating outer clutter. Delving into your inner processes lights up your path to clarity.

DEVELOPING AN
ENLIGHTENED INNER SELF

Organizing your inner self and your well-being is about the removal of any negativity, past wounds, and emotional blocks, coupled with becoming healthy and authentically happy, with a great attitude, and optimal communication skills. When your inner self is not organized, and you are without a clear sense of being, your surroundings will always be chaotic. That being said, no matter how disorganized you are, you will be able to get organized with insight into your inner self.

Even the most organized people have blips into a disorganized state but will recover quickly by noticing and rectifying self-defeating cluttering behavior. Perhaps the self-defeating behavior starts by placing a reminder on a bare kitchen counter, then a magazine finds its way on top of the reminder note, followed by collections of random and unrelated items. Meanwhile, a large lump of clothes begins to grow on the bedroom chair, waiting to be relocated to the closet. So, when you personally start to get wayward, something is more than likely going on with you internally for this ungovernable chaos to rise up. You will not eliminate moments of disorganization, but by having a specific home for everything you own and using the strategies and the steps you're going to learn, you will recover to an organized state quickly and with ease.

A systemic approach for a satisfying space, and understanding your stuff, is achieved by connecting to your inner self, dreams, interests, and goals, and learning to symbolize aggregated collections. Once you realize the deeper meaning to everything you own, what you love to do in life, and what makes life worth living, then, and only then, will you know what "good" stuff to keep around versus what is simply clutter. Your life purpose helps you understand what material objects are useful, purposeful, sentimental, and loved. Investing in a peaceful, tranquil, orderly, and sustainable strategy for decluttering comes from being self-aware and patient with the changes that will take place. The physical aspect of getting organized happens rapidly, yet the preparation internally takes thoughtfulness, tenacity, and strategizing. Ultimately, revealing to yourself what you love to do in life will help you understand what you love about your stuff versus what is simply cluttering your life.

NO JUDGMENT:
BE HONEST AND KIND WITH YOURSELF

Decluttering effectively requires self-honesty, since the goal is to remove from your home whatever is inauthentic, out of date, and burying or blocking your authentic self and aspirations. As you do, little and big gems of understanding will fall into your lap, astounding and dazzling you. Clearing up hazy half-truths and stupefying, self-defeating behaviors clears the path to becoming a champion and builder of your empire.

Ironically, one of the things people discover is how they could have fooled or misled themselves about their own lives, often with good intentions, yet in very unsettling ways. Santa Claus and the Tooth Fairy are innocent, well-meaning untruths, but as a child I remember feeling a little squeamish when I realized I had been duped. Since then, it's made me wonder: Do these early fictions teach us that it's okay and sometimes preferred to lie and dupe ourselves? To tell "little white lies" or say yes when we want to say no? To pick a career that does not interest us because parents or society convince us that it is the only way to succeed? Or to choose a particular path because we think it will be the only thing we will be good at? Are we supposed to deny what we enjoy because others will judge us or we believe it's wrong? When people are confused about what they want in life, the Clutter Remedy is an excellent process for recognizing personal truth.

For this reason, I always advise people to approach declutter-ing from the stance of "no judgment." See clearly, be honest, and avoid blame. Foster unconditional love and regard for yourself. Be kind, no matter what you discover. By going through this pro-cess, you've committed to remedying the accumulated clutter in your space, and this usually requires seeing and addressing your inner clutter: the issues, emotions, pain, and untruths that led to it. No one, including yourself, is allowed to judge you, criticize you, or complain about how much you own, how you collected it, or what you will keep. No one should be eyeing your stuff for themselves. It's your stuff and nobody else's business. Accepting your clutter as you find it, without feeling shame or regret, is the optimal stance. This will help you see more clearly and will help you recognize any negative patterns and attitudes that you will want to work through prior to going through all your stuff. Fo-cusing on blame and getting mired in judgment will only stress you out and bog you down.

One thing that helps make the experience fun and uplifting is to remember that everything you own was chosen for a reason. You acquired things with good intentions; they were useful or they served a purpose or you simply loved them. So when you look at your possessions objectively, ask yourself, "Why is this in my real estate? Why did I think this was a good idea?" You could have chosen certain items because they reminded you of good times. Or they were expensive items that conveyed a certain sta-tus you desired. We buy and keep items for lots of reasons. Some items you find during decluttering will remain useful and serve a purpose and still be loved, while some will make no sense at all. Remaining nonjudgmental and enthusiastic rather than ashamed and befuddled over your stuff is easier when you see how it relates to your core values. Remember, the goal of decluttering is to cre-ate an organized, satisfying, and productive lifestyle.

DEFINING YOUR UNIQUE CORE VALUES

Reflecting on what you truly value, and absorbing what your current life interests are, is the beginning and most important step to getting organized and knowing what to keep in your life. It's a big deal and can feel daunting to articulate what you value in life. Before going through the decluttering process, ask yourself, "What do I love to do in life? What are my core values?"

Delving into your personal world helps you understand your personal effects and how they align with your life. Do you value relationships, children, money, power, career, fame, independence, travel, sleep, appearance, health, and/or spirituality?

To help identify what you truly want out of life, make a list of your top ten core values. For example, the core values you name could be intimacy, an ideal partner, relaxation, friendship, family time, optimal health, creativity, and a thriving business. They could include vacation time, increased income, particular hobbies, an ideal career, or an ideal social life.

Figuring out the top ten things you value will motivate you to make changes and to get organized. For instance, if you long for a relationship leading to marriage and children, but you will not invite a new person to your tangled home, are you ready to go forward with a relationship? Or do you value your independence more? If you value rest and sleep, why is there an abundance of stuff on your bed, so much so that you sack out on a bumpy couch instead? If you value travel, why are your receipts and paperwork for your taxes buried all over your home, leaving you hesitant to spend money on a vacation? If you value expanding your business, why is your office and your company car filled with junk mail, papers, unpacked boxes, and yesterday's dry cleaning?

After naming ten core values, next make certain they reflect the aspirations that are most meaningful to you in your current life. Are they past desires, or what someone else wants for you, or things you believe you *should* value? You're the only one who knows what you want out of life.

Now memorize your top ten core values, and contemplate what your life would look like with those ten core values developed and manifested in your life. Obviously, you want your values to align with your capabilities and be achievable, but reach high and imagine your wildest and most extraordinary dreams at this very moment. Now make a strong wish to have the top ten values fulfilled. Ask for these wishes to become present in your life. Write each of your top ten values as goals, and write three specific ways you will fulfill each one of them. Create a timeline to achieve them.

Values guide us in every aspect of our lives. Knowing your core values when choosing friends, a career, where to live, whether to have kids, how to raise kids, and what kind of home and lifestyle you want is key to getting what you truly want.

Focus on what you want without focusing on the inconsistencies between where you are in your current life situation and what you want for your future. Paint a vivid picture of your *ideal* lifestyle. If you value good health, what would a healthy lifestyle look like? What food would you eat? What kind of exercise would you do, and how often would you do it? If you value good friends, how would you find them? What would you plan to do with them, and what would you talk about? If you value furthering your career, how would you secure an interview? What kind of preparation would you make for the interview? How far would you be willing to travel? If you want a partner in life, how would you find them? What traits would you look for? What criteria would you have for an ideal partner?

By defining what you value, and imagining your ideal lifestyle, you create goals and a vision to aspire to. This will help inspire the hard work it will take to become and stay organized.

You are giving yourself the freedom to create and enjoy the life you've always dreamed of. Yet know that lasting change requires strong motivation and willpower. Working on yourself before your space prepares you for the physical, emotional, and mental aspects of getting organized. It isn't always easy to align what's important to you with your actions, to create consistency in behavior for the pursuit of happiness, peace, tranquility, and excitement in our everyday life. But the minute you write down goals, take time to focus on them and make them happen. Goals are not meant to stay on paper; they are meant to write your life story.

Usually, being organized is not something someone will put on their top ten list of core values, but it is something everyone values to a certain degree. It will help inspire you to work harder on the decluttering process. Going from a so-so lifestyle to something grander and more opulent is exceptionally easy when you understand it's attainable by using your imagination and when you don't let clutter get in the way of your vision.

MAKING YOUR SECRET DREAMS AND ASPIRATIONS COME TRUE

For a variety of reasons, you can resist talking about your dreams and life goals. Perhaps you think they are unrealistic or you don't feel worthy. Yet revealing any secret dreams is important in order to accurately assess your belongings and clear them out of your space. Stuffing dreams down inside often leads to stuffing up your life with things that don't enhance, but rather thwart, your current life from moving forward. Secret dreams may involve building an empire or becoming an actor, writer, athlete, singer, or dancer. People often never mention their secret dreams even to a partner, a family member, or their closest friends. Secret dreams float around in everyone's mind at some time or another. They could be about wanting to get married, leaving a relationship, or traveling to a faraway place. Secret dreams could be about quitting a job and having down time. When people don't articulate their innermost desires, it's as if they are building a wall to keep their dreams from escaping into reality. Whatever is true for you, this is the time to be the conductor of your own well-orchestrated life.

Joan collected everything to do with horses. As a child she had dreamed of owning and riding horses, and in lieu of ever doing that she started collecting horse figurines, which as an adult she continued to display throughout her home. In adulthood, Joan started to buy equestrian clothing and equipment, such as stirrup pants, cowboy boots, hats, saddles, and horseshoes. Though she secretly held on to her childhood dreams and still fantasized about living an equestrian lifestyle, the only thing she did to pursue it was to collect more stuff. After Joan did an assessment of her current lifestyle, she realized she had thwarted and ignored her dream of being an equestrian. At first Joan thought the answer to her clutter challenge would mean getting rid of her horse collections, but after admitting her dreams out loud, she realized the opposite. Not only did she want to keep her stuff, but she began to actively pursue an equestrian lifestyle, which improved her life immensely. Joan found a horse she could afford and started riding lessons, and soon she found a "cowboy" boyfriend to go line dancing with. She enjoyed and loved all her collections again and began regularly using her riding gear. Joan started volunteering with therapy horses and then teaching her grandkids how to ride, which became one of the most fulfilling dreams she could pursue.

Emilio had always dreamed of being a champion tennis player, and when I met him, he had an overaccumulation of tennis gear, including twenty-two tennis rackets and closets filled with tennis clothes and shoes. However, he rarely played tennis. He did not exercise, practice, or meet with a tennis coach regularly. Most of his time was spent working to support his family and hanging out with his friends.

Emilio loved the idea of being a tennis star, and he entered a few tennis tournaments, but he never won. He did not have the physical stamina, technique, or discipline to practice for hours and hours every week. Emilio's coaches told him he did not have the hand-eye coordination, balance, or timing it takes to be a great player. No matter what he was told, Emilio still believed he was going to be a professional tennis player, and he initially insisted on keeping all his tennis gear for his "future victories."

In truth, Emilio did not want to face his own disappointment over not achieving his tennis dreams. Over time, Emilio started to search for a new sport to enjoy and excel in. After much introspection, Emilio discovered golf, which was much more in line with his particular athletic abilities. Emilio's new passion and focus on golf helped him clear out all his tennis gear, which he donated to charity. In its place Emilio purchased a new golf wardrobe and golf equipment, and he made a point of only purchasing what he would use regularly, what served a purpose, and things he loved. He acknowledged overcollecting did not equate to excelling in something.

The point of these stories is that making major changes in your life is not as important as feeling happy, enthusiastic, and productive. Changing is something you want to do or don't want to do. When change is something you want, do it in small steps, with competence, and have a deadline to accomplish your goals. You don't want to jump off the high dive when you haven't learned how to swim well. Creating a world that is safe, economically sound, and in harmony with your qualifications, proficiencies, desires, and goals takes discipline, determination, planning, and follow-through. Getting a clear read on where you stand currently helps you plan the future you want to achieve. Doing the next exercise will help you understand your current self better. When you understand your inner self better, you will understand everything in your life better, especially your clutter.

CURRENT LIFE-STATUS INVENTORY

Next, create what I call your "current life-status inventory," which is your individual current life picture. Living your ideal lifestyle means taking a considerable look into your current one. This inventory helps you determine if you have settled for a less-than-ideal life. When you look at your current life on paper, you can come to realize that it is "dated," like some of the old clothes and electronics you still own. You can realize you feel trapped, like some projects you stuffed away under the bed. You can have thoughts locked in your head that indicate you "don't deserve anything better." You could have adopted a steady and secure lifestyle in order to not "rock the boat." Getting a baseline of your current life status helps you develop what you want now and for the future. Answering the nine questions below helps prepare you for the balance it takes to become perpetually organized.

1. Where do you live? Who do you live with?
2. Do you work? If so, where?
3. Are you happy or unhappy about the above situations? Explain.
4. Who are you, and what are you about? What do you do in life?
5. What do you do for fun and/or relaxation?
6. Name the closest people in your life. Do they bring you happiness? Why or why not?
7. Briefly explain how well you are doing in the following areas:

    • Relationships
    • Mental health
    • Emotions
    • Physical health

- Social life
- Money
- Culture / beliefs about life

8. What are you doing to improve in or change about the above areas?

9. Which five positive feelings or emotions would you like to experience more often?

Improving your life takes some digging around in places that are complex and painful. I won't beat around the bush on that. A great life doesn't magically happen. Inducing marvel, instead of stupor, in your life takes a plan of action and a bold trek into anything that will get in your way. Any past negative experiences that still cause you pain may not always be recognizable, unless you get real with parts of yourself that have gone by the wayside. There may be younger, wounded aspects of yourself you have buried and not dealt with. An ideal lifestyle is only as ideal as you make it, and it occurs when your emotional clutter is cleared and healed.

RECOGNIZING AND HEALING PAST WOUNDS

The most difficult emotions that arise during decluttering and organizing often relate to traumatic or hurtful incidents that happened in the past. People don't realize the connection between the past and the present since they believe they "got over" those past events years ago. However, emotional scars can be persistent and enduring. They don't disappear, poof, all gone, just because we wish them away or say so. Painful events can stay with us and well up at the most inconvenient time. Sometimes people say they "got over" or "got past" things, but what they mean is that they ignored and buried the pain, believing that time alone would heal those wounds. As most people eventually learn, emotions don't work this way. Instead, blocking and stuffing pain only defers our experience of it, and those feelings can blow up in our face at any given moment, blinding us, and send us heading for a fall. Experiences you put "behind" you will eventually chase you down. Healing takes both time and focused effort. It doesn't happen on its own.

Confronting clutter can trigger old wounds. When it is approached willingly, by facing those wounds, it can lead to a cathartic experience through which you release the pain and suffering for good. This first means acknowledging and feeling your emotions, and no longer holding them in, and this may involve tears, crying, and expressing and expelling negative emotions in a curative and beneficial way. To get all of the angst and trauma out, you want to pull out pain by the roots.

Clearing and Healing Strategy

A great strategy for clearing up emotional clutter and healing any past trauma is what I call a "clearing and healing strategy." This is a way to have inner communication with past parts of yourself. It starts by listing five of your most common negative emotions, those dark feelings you experience on a regular basis. Feel those emotions and remember when those awful feelings first started. Identify how old that part of yourself was. It could be a very young self or an older past part of yourself. Now visualize the image of your younger self, in your mind's eye, and then project that image in the room with you. See that younger self as clearly as possible: How are they dressed? How is their hair styled? How are they sitting or standing? Then introduce yourself to your younger self, and share the good things about your life now, along with what is different from the past.

Dialogue with your younger self. Ask them, "What do you think about that?" Listen for their answer; don't think for them.

Then ask the younger self, "How are you doing?" Again, listen for their answer, and don't be tempted to think of the answer in your head. The younger self will answer, reminding you of what hurt them. Reassure your younger self that whatever happened was not their fault, and while whatever happened was wrong, it is not happening anymore. Ask your younger self what they want from your adult self, and then fulfill their reasonable requests. Typically, the younger part wants to know that you are okay and that things turned out well in spite of their own distressing and disturbing experiences. Reassuring the younger self that you survived those difficult times and are in a completely different stage of life will help your younger self move on and heal.

Dealing with clutter and organizing your life often means dealing with the places where you are still stuck or struggling with past distressing memories. In this situation, your younger self will want to know that you are willing to work on healing the lingering angst created in the past. As you organize your space, it is important to let your wounded younger self know that you don't want their help with the clutter. Indeed, assure them that you don't want their help in any part of your current adult life. Once you help all your younger selves heal, tell them to "be free" and to "go have fun."

This technique of inner communication can also be used to heal unresolved wounds and conflicts with other people, particularly those who have died or whom you can't or don't want to speak to directly. Simply visualize meeting these difficult or unavailable people using your imagination, and communicate with them. Visualize a comfortable room with a mediator or neutral party who will help you work on a resolution. Discuss whatever unresolved and unfinished business you have with the person, express any negative emotions, and share whatever insight you have about why certain things occurred.

The goal is to have a cathartic release of pain and suffering in a loving, safe, and unconditional manner. This exercise takes focus and some time to get used to, but it provides insight into other people and your life in a nonthreatening way. It is a safe way to confront, understand, and forgive people who have hurt you or to communicate with people you have lost. Ultimately, the aim is to understand and heal any lingering confusion, hatred, shame, and remorse from past relationships, so that you have the emotional freedom to pursue your ideal life in the present.

RECOGNIZING YOUR SPIRITUAL BELIEF SYSTEM

Part of creating your ideal life means understanding your personal beliefs and organizing your lifestyle in alignment with them. I believe that an organized healthy self, one focused on all aspects of wellness, includes one's belief system. I like to think of humans as spiritual beings in a physical experience. We are Soul. Soul is from one source, split off into creative sparks of light, carried by a current of sound into a physical body. I believe, at all times, our physical form is linked by a silver cord to the original source. Therefore, we have an inner resource of wisdom, connectivity, and power at all times. We have all the answers within for any challenges we face.

You may give your philosophies, theories, and spiritual beliefs a lot of thought, and they are firm and clear, or you may not think about them at all. Perhaps you ascribe to a particular religious or spiritual path or you don't. It's also okay to move about in your ideas and thoughts until you have some awareness of who you are and life's deeper meaning is clear to you. Only you know what you believe in at any given moment. However, when you find yourself clueless or uncertain about your existence, I encourage you to take the time to consider these questions and to ponder the larger meaning of life. This is part of being grounded in your life's larger purpose in order to stay organized. Having awareness of who you are and your true purpose is one of the greatest gifts you will experience and share with others.

Take a few moments to reflect on and answer these questions:

- Do you believe in a higher power? Are you not sure?
- Do you believe in an organized religion? A spiritual path?
- Do you have a savior or a master you follow?
- Do you believe in evolution? Are you agnostic or atheist?
- Do you believe wholeheartedly in a specific doctrine, or do you have your own theories?

Whatever you believe in helps you become clearer about yourself and what you value in life. An unclear spiritual path leads to an unclear physical environment, a bumpier road, and an undeniable confusion about everything, including who to include in your life.

DEVELOPING A POSITIVE
SOCIAL SUPPORT SYSTEM

Knowing how to evaluate and understand who will be great in your life and who will not is not always easy, especially when they are family, old friends, neighbors, and coworkers. There are many ways to determine who stays and who goes. Hurtful people create drama, affecting and impacting you on all levels, physically, mentally, and emotionally. I always say, "Like attracts like," so getting clarity on those you want in your life will help clear out the people you don't want in your life. Some people can be considered "life clutter."

Befriending people with similar values makes life flow better.

Running around with a wild party crowd when you're introspective or in recovery leads to misery. Staying home, isolated and alone, when you value the limelight will engulf you in sadness and despondency. Surrounding yourself with people who have conflicting ideas and philosophies may be great in a debate, but it's not great in your personal life. Being involved with unfavorable people is as damaging as living in clutter. Eliminating from your life any people with ill will is always a good idea.

Establishing strong boundaries with people who rely on you too much, who are not reciprocal, and who do not have your best interest at heart is in your best interest. Communicating clearly with yourself and with other people will keep balance in all areas of your life, and being a clear communicator will ultimately make clearing your space so much easier and effective. As I discuss next, improving communication skills is the most intriguing part of clearing clutter from your life.

2

CHANGING YOUR LANGUAGE WILL CHANGE YOUR LIFE

Changing how you communicate will help increase your productivity, timeliness, and creative life processes and allow you to live an organized life. The number-one cause of perpetual disorganization is the use of what I call "impeding language." The way you talk to yourself and others directly impacts your behavior, along with cluttered corners, cabinets, and packed and erratic spaces. Impeding language leads to overcollecting, overaccumulating, and cluttering in the most insidious and derailing ways.

ELIMINATING IMPEDING LANGUAGE FROM YOUR LIFE

Distinguishing wants from needs, using decisive language and eliminating indecisive language, and putting adjectives or feeling

words and the word *will* back into your language assures you of
having ease with the decluttering process. Changing your language will also improve your productivity and help you fulfill
your goals before, during, and after the decluttering process.

I believe "I need" is the most overused phrase in our language. We say "I need" all the time: I need to get out of here; I
need to pick up the kids; I need to call that guy; I need to do something with my hair; I need to exercise; I need new clothes; I need a
new car. I need, I need, I need! This phrase comes up often during
the decluttering process. Someone holds up item after item and
says, "I need this." But the truth is, "I need" is a white lie. Saying
you need something that is not an essential need instead of saying
you "want" something or that you will "do" something is a way to
avoid recognizing or admitting that you are making a choice, and
it will disrupt you from remaining organized and productive. We
are in essence "needling" ourselves to death. Needling yourself
to do things instead of willing yourself to do things is the barrier
to follow-through. Needling is the cause of tension, worry, and
nervousness.

I believe we only have seven essential needs: air, food, water,
shelter, sleep, elimination, and sunlight. These are the seven things
that keep us alive. Nothing else is a need. Misusing the phrase "I
need" is what often leads to overcollecting and overaccumulation
to begin with. It leads to overshopping and stockpiling stuff to
degrees that are neither useful nor purposeful. This disorganized
way of thinking leads to disorganized clutter and often neglect of
one's actual needs. A clutter-filled, nonfunctioning home gets in
the way of sufficient sleep, balanced nourishment, proper hydra-
tion, fresh air, detoxifying eliminations, sufficient sunlight, and
optimal shelter. Misusing the word *need* will also make it much
more difficult to declutter and stay organized.

In general, listen to others and keep track of how many times
you hear people say some version of "I need," such as "I must,"

"I have to," or "I gotta." How often do these phrases pertain to the necessities that keep us alive? More importantly, as you go through the decluttering process, listen to yourself and stop every time you hear yourself say, "I need this item." Even when the item is used for one of the essential needs, rephrase to say, "I am choosing to keep this because…" Clarify why you're making that choice; evaluate how it fits with your core values. Ask yourself: "Is it useful? Does it serve a purpose? Is it sentimental? Do I love it?"

For instance, we need food. But the kind of food we eat, and where and how we get it, is a choice. Most people shop for food in grocery stores, but you don't *need* to. Some people grow their own food and hunt, while some people never cook, eating solely in restaurants. You also don't *need* to pay your taxes. Not paying them will not kill you, though eventually you will find yourself in serious trouble with the IRS. That won't kill you either, but it can lead to financial disaster and legal challenges. For this reason, people usually *choose* to pay their taxes to avoid those negative consequences.

You can view this change to your language as semantics, but it's not. When you deliberately make conscious choices — by saying "I want" or "I will" rather than "I need" — you emphasize the positive reasons, values, and motivations that are important to you. This helps keep you from feeling trapped by obligations. For example, if you have children, you are regularly choosing how to care for them. You don't "have" to buy them certain toys or pick them up from school if you don't want to. They won't die if you don't buy them things or if you fail to show up. Of course, you want them to be happy and get home safely, yet there are other ways of achieving all that: fun activities instead of more stuff, earning their own money to buy things, taking a bus or public transit, sharing a ride with someone else, and walking or biking themselves. It is important to know that nothing you do is a "have to," unless it is one of the seven actual needs.

Sometimes, admitting that you don't want to do something will lead to clever solutions. Or perhaps, even though after-school pickups are an annoying chore, you *will* do it because you want to love and care for your kids. However, you also can decide that certain responsibilities and roles are incongruent with your ideal life, and even abhorrent, and you will choose not to do those things to pursue what you enjoy instead. Once you rid yourself of "I need," the freedom of life begins. You choose to fulfill your actual needs in numerous ways — in how you breathe, what you eat and drink, the home you live in, the clothing you wear, your sleep habits, how you care for the body, plus getting enough sun. Realizing that fulfilling your actual needs involves hundreds of choices, and that you're in charge of making them, makes life a whole lot sweeter and more enjoyable.

Consciously *choosing* to declutter and get organized makes the process easier, too. Remember: You don't "need" to get rid of anything, and you don't "need" to keep anything. Make everything a choice that serves the larger purpose of your life.

INDECISIVE LANGUAGE
VERSUS DECISIVE LANGUAGE

After "I need," the most common phrase I hear when helping people get perpetually organized is "I'll try": I'll try to get organized; I'll try to finish this weekend; I'll try to keep the kitchen and the house clean from now on; I'll try not to buy so much stuff anymore. I call this type of impeding language "indecisive language."

Indecisive language keeps you chained to your clutter. It makes decision-making impossible. Using decisive language helps you fulfill your dreams and goals. "I'll try" or "I tried" signals indecision, doubt, resistance, reluctance, or fear. It expresses a lack of commitment or self-confidence. If you hear yourself saying "I'll try" as you go through this process, recognize this as expressing indecision about getting organized. Know that you either will or won't accomplish your goals. Don't "try" to succeed. Be decisive. Saying "I'll try" indicates nonaction; it means nothing.

When people don't finish something they set out to do, they often say "I tried" as a way to excuse themselves or escape blame. For instance, when someone misses an appointment, they say, "I tried to get to my doctor's office today," as if making the attempt is what's important. It is a way to blame circumstances instead of taking responsibility for not following through on goals you set for yourself: "I tried, but there was traffic," "I lost track of time," or "I took an important phone call." Do those reasons matter? Not when it comes to following through and accomplishing tasks. The appointment was missed, and the person did not see the doctor. That someone "tried" does not change the outcome.

The same is true of decluttering and organizing your space. When you only get partway through the process and stop, your home will remain cluttered and disorganized, and most likely, any progress you make will be riddled with indecision. Again, this is more than semantics; the use of impeding language will jeopardize going forward toward a positive outcome. In addition to "I'll try," listen for these other indecisive phrases: I might, I may, maybe, but, probably, perhaps, we'll see, someday, sometime, somehow, if, could, should, possibly, not necessarily, and I'll think about it. Finally, the two most popular indecisive words, which I hear constantly, are "kinda" and "sorta." To increase their impact, these are often combined as "kinda sorta" or "sorta kinda." Imagine that, two new phrases that mean nothing are now cluttering how we speak. I recently spoke to a woman who used "kinda" and "sorta" in every sentence, saying, "I kinda sorta need to get organized." How much more indecisive could she be?

You will improve organizational success by setting clear goals and committing to them. One thing that helps is specifying a time frame. Say, "I will get organized within the month." Eliminating indecisive language will help you become more decisive about what to keep and what not to keep and what to do and what not to do. When decluttering, some items can be put into the "projects" category. These are items you have uncertainty about, which you will work on down the road, and therefore they become "to dos." Decisive language also helps you express how you feel, decisively.

EMOTIONAL CLARITY: IDENTIFYING YOUR FEELINGS

The decluttering process is sometimes like pulling a rose bush out of the dirt with your bare hands. You will encounter thorns — in the form of prickly and uncomfortable feelings. In essence, in order to eliminate emotional clutter and successfully organize your space, you will want to pull out those thorns as you work. That means acknowledging emotions as they surface, correctly labeling and understanding them, and then healing any lingering hurt or pain.

One challenge people face during the decluttering process is that they are not familiar with their own feelings, in general. Serious clutter often occurs because someone is actively ignoring or avoiding certain difficult emotions or feelings stemming from past traumatic events. When this is the case, uncovering, understanding, and healing those emotions is part of the process (see "Clearing and Healing Strategy," pages 26–28).

Only you know what you feel. Only you can say when negative feelings are blocking you from moving ahead, what those feelings are, and where they come from. Others can help — by listening and providing support and insight — but they can't do it for you. This is the same as decluttering itself: Supportive people will help you carry and move stuff around, and offer advice about your space, but it's up to you to decide what to keep, donate, gift, or sell and where to put everything, based on how often and where you use things. Ideally, the decluttering process will be a healing experience rather than a tenacious upheaval, and it will help you recognize and cope with any negative feelings that are keeping you from blossoming.

A good place to start is to ask yourself, "How do I feel about the clutter?" Ask yourself this question before you start, and ask it again during the process. As you do, see if your answer changes or becomes clearer.

You can feel hopeless or hopeful, discontent or excited, depending on how you view clutter and what you want to do about it. When questioned or pressured about clutter, you can feel upset and claim you "don't care" about the clutter. How you answer that question will determine what you want to do to pull out any negative emotional thorns. When you say you don't care about the clutter, that is apathy. Sometimes when I ask people how they feel about their clutter, they are insulted and become defensive, claiming they "don't care about getting organized." They claim to be apathetic, which is a very common feeling and reaction today. But in my experience, when people answer by saying, "I don't care," that is the opposite of the truth. The mess represents a situation they care about very deeply, and their defensive stubbornness has become a stumbling block to fixing it. Sometimes, people feign apathy to hide disappointment or shame over what they perceive as past failure. They are protecting themselves behind an "I don't care" wall and are afraid of what will happen, and what they will feel, when they take it down. Indeed, their clutter has become a physical wall, and they resist removing it for the same reason they built their emotional wall — fear of being disappointed and hurt by their circumstances. Their emotions can in turn be bigger than their clutter. This is why it's important to build a bridge to reach your dreams and clear a path to your ideal lifestyle. Taking down walls and clearing your space for a clearer understanding of what you want and knowing what you feel passionate about is the beginning of living your ideal life.

Another issue that can transpire during decluttering is having difficulty identifying your feelings or mislabeling them. Using, instead of grasping for, the correct words when you have an intense emotional reaction is key to expressing your feelings. Our language has many adjectives, or feeling words, that can be used to name exact feelings. Not using accurate adjectives will keep you stopped up and will easily stop the process of decluttering. Feelings are like nature, and you want to make sense of your varied emotions as they flood in. When I ask people what they are feeling, they sometimes say, "I don't know," and they mean it. Our vocabulary for feeling words has depleted to a few simple terms, such as *overwhelmed*, *frustrated*, *upset*, *angry*, or *sad*, and that's it.

When negative and positive emotions flare up, put them into descriptive terms. Instead of saying "I feel that..." or "I feel like...," say "I feel..." and follow it with a feeling word. When you start a sentence with "I feel that..." or "I feel like...," and express a thought instead of verbalizing a feeling, you are actively suppressing whatever emotions you are feeling, and you are also using impeding language. For help describing and identifying your innermost feelings as specifically as possible, use a "Feeling Chart" (which you can find at www.i-deal-lifestyle.com/feeling-chart.html). There are hundreds and hundreds of adjectives to describe how you feel, but you use only a handful of them. If you're "upset" or "angry," specify in what way and for what reason. Are you furious, devastated, afraid, or over-the-top enraged?

When people are disconnected from their feelings, or avoid their feelings, and don't know how to name them, this leads to cluttered and clogged emotions and confused understandings. When you don't know what you feel, you will not be clear on what you think or what to do; this is true in any given situation and especially while decluttering.

Conversely, when you know how you feel, you will know exactly what to do, as long as you are motivated to make changes in your life. Feelings don't lie. Emotional waves are like nature; they just keep coming. During the decluttering process, you will make hundreds of decisions, big and small, which is why understanding your feelings is so important. If at any time you struggle making decisions about stuff, the best way to figure things out is to ask, "How do I feel?" Brainstorming or bouncing ideas off others will help you get clearer on what you feel, think, and know.

By recognizing any negativity that's blocking you, labeling feelings accurately, and working through them, you will declutter your emotions and your thoughts and begin to view your things, your space, and your life in a positive way. The more skilled you become at describing and understanding your feelings, the better you will become at understanding and organizing your stuff.

As you evaluate objects, lots of memories and feelings from the past will bubble up, and some could surprise you: longing, guilt, confusion, anxiety, love, regret, affection. You will also discover that once-beloved items and activities no longer hold any interest at all. You will recognize unconscious behavioral patterns related to what you keep and how you care for your things. In short, you will come to understand yourself, your feelings, and your aspirations in new and practical ways.

Clarifying Emotions and Language
Will Clarify Clutter

When Fiona became a grandmother, she took up knitting, crochet, and needlepoint. She bought oodles of yarn, needles, and gadgets for her crafts, and she enjoyed making sweaters and artwork for her children and grandchildren. For about five years, she reveled in these art forms, and then as the grandkids got older, she grew tired of these projects. After ten years, Fiona realized that these crafts no longer matched her current hankerings and ambitions, and she felt vexed by them. She was more interested in playing bridge and golf and traveling, and she discovered she never wanted to knit, crochet, or needlepoint ever again. And yet all her yarn, needles, and gadgets were still around, taking up an entire bedroom closet of her apartment. So as she evaluated her things and reinvented and reorganized her space, Fiona decided to donate all these once-important craft items to a worthy charity.

When it's time for you to start looking through your bric-a-brac, it can be very difficult to decipher clutter from worthy items, especially in a crowded, disordered space. This is why I suggest clarifying your values and ideal life before you start, since these will help guide you to make good decisions. However, that won't make it any easier emotionally. As you declutter, you can become filled with heavy thoughts and negative emotions. You could become disappointed, melancholy, or grief-stricken. Whenever this happens, it's best to pause, recognize these difficult feelings, and clear and cope with them before continuing; this way, you will stay on task and declutter effectively. Don't rush. Approach this process like an opportunity to explore your inner self, along with your space, and be open to any revelations that come out of the clutter. The contents of your space will tell you a lot about what's going on inside, and your inner self will let you know what stuff truly resonates with you.

Getting organized won't last if it's done because someone thinks it is the "correct" or popular thing to do. Staying organized is only possible when it serves someone's larger life goals or values. But even then, perpetual organization can be undermined by cluttered emotions, unclear thinking, and indecisiveness, which are reflected in how you talk. So before, during, and after the decluttering and organizing process, gently correct your language and self-talk. This doesn't happen overnight. But even though it can take a while to master, revising your everyday language will change your life and get you off the "human in a hamster wheel" round-and-round cycle for good.

Consistently avoid the word *need* except for one of the seven life-sustaining areas. Work fervently to learn new words that express your feelings, which will help free you up from negativity and remorse. Stop saying "I'll try," which often leads to procrastination, lack of follow-through, and lack of drive. Instead, say "I will," which improves relationships, increases productivity and effectiveness, and reflects confidence. Say, "I will finish the project by Tuesday," "I will do the laundry," "I will be on time for work." Putting *will* back into your everyday language inspires decisive action. The removal of the word *will* from your language is the main reason for procrastination, failure to follow through, and lack of drive. I believe impeding language is responsible for a decline in human incentive, ambition, and determination to follow through, as well as a decrease in productivity levels, widespread, perpetual excuses, hesitancy to step up, and the dodging of common responsibilities.

WORKING WITH OTHERS:
LANGUAGE AND RELATIONSHIPS

A good strategy for gently correcting your language is to find a "language partner" who understands and wants to join you in this practice. Working together, you can correct each other's impeding language and be supportive. When done in a reciprocal, fun way, instead of an insulting and demeaning way, it makes for a faster learning curve. In general, people don't like to be corrected and criticized for the words they use, so don't correct other people if they haven't explicitly joined you in this practice. Focus instead on yourself. However, as you become more aware of your own everyday language, you will hear how common negative, self-defeating talk is with everyone: parents, teachers, loved ones, bosses, and friends. In a way, you, I, and everyone else are programmed to use impeding language, and now is your chance to turn it around and create a way to speak that empowers you to live the most ideal and well-run lifestyle you've ever imagined.

Additionally, checking in with others about what they feel, think, and know is important for having authentic relationships. When you don't ask others direct questions, you will not know — at all — what others are going through. So many misconceptions can occur for yourself and others when thoughts, feelings, and knowledge are not shared. Don't hesitate to figure out what is the truth in every situation and how you feel about it. Feeling misunderstood by others starts with misunderstanding yourself. Misunderstanding yourself leads to misunderstanding others and your environment. Clarifying and verbalizing what you think versus what you know, and sharing your thoughts and feelings, will help make your life and relationships easier. Sputtering, squashing, or shelving feelings, thoughts, and knowledge creates emotional stoppage instead of free will. Your clutter then becomes a symbol of your cluttered self.

Resolving Conflicts: Assertive Language and Validation Tool

In shared living situations, decluttering and organizing will ideally include the cooperation and involvement of everyone in the house. However, sometimes people who live together are in conflict and this isn't possible. People will disagree over who's to blame for the clutter, what to do about it, and how to organize things. Or fights over clutter can be arguments about something else. The most common sources of relationship conflict are money, sex, moral issues, parenting, children, pets, and housekeeping.

Since successfully organizing a home often requires resolving these conflicts and disagreements, do so using this assertive language and validation tool. Also seek the help of a Clutter Remedy organizer and/or a qualified relationship expert. A neutral third party can sometimes help everyone find a way to compromise.

First of all, everyone is allowed to share negative feelings, and everyone is allowed to be heard. But how people speak to one another can make all the difference in finding resolutions that satisfy everyone. When sharing negative feelings, claim those feelings as your own, rather than blame others for causing them. Be specific about the problem and what you want to change. Express caring for others while validating their feelings and intentions. And finally, ask others to share their perspective and feelings. In essence, speak to others in the same caring, understanding, open ways that you want them to speak to you.

Here are some positive and negative examples of what this will sound like. Imagine a couple in which one person is frustrated by a mess that is largely made by the other person. Using assertive language and validation, the frustrated person can say:

> I feel upset about the piles of paper all over the living room. I would like the papers to be moved elsewhere, so the living room remains neat. I know you work hard and often get home late, and you are too tired to pick things up. I love you and know that you have good intentions and want an orderly home, too. How do you feel, and what do you think we will do?

In this example, the person first describes their feelings using an "I" statement, rather than a "you" statement (such as, "you make me upset when..."). Using assertive language, they describe the reason for those feelings and the preferred solution. Then they shift to validation: They express caring and understanding of the other person, validate their good intentions, and ask the other person to share their own feelings and their own perspective.

Now imagine two different responses by the other person. The first is a negative example of nonassertive language and a lack of validation:

> You are always upset about something. A little mess doesn't make any difference. I want to relax when I get home, and I can't change the way I am. Do what you want, but I think you are way too picky.

Obviously, this would be a very upsetting response! Why? First, the person dismisses the problem itself and invalidates the other person's feelings. Using "you," they blame the other for causing the conflict. Also, the person is only thinking about what they want and not what is good for all.

In contrast, here is a positive example of an assertive, validating response:

> I don't want you to be upset about clutter or upset with me. I am not bothered by the papers, but since you are, I will change to keep the house neater. I love you and want you to be happy. Since I am tired at night, what if I put my things in a particular place and organize them in the morning?

What's important to note here is that, even though the other person still doesn't experience the mess as a problem, they validate their partner's feelings and perspective and present a specific solution that will work for both of them.

Even when someone responds defensively, do not change your approach or communication style by becoming aggressive or passive. Continue to use assertive, validating language. Even when a particular problem can't be immediately resolved, you will become more assertive in a respectful way and start to establish and maintain your boundaries. That said, also be alert for signs that someone is irate about something else. In the negative example above, the person exaggerates the problem by saying, "You are always upset." Extreme statements that use "never" and "always," in which someone makes a mountain out of a molehill, can indicate underlying challenges or negative feelings the person has stuffed away. So do open hostility, unreasonable demands, unfair accusations, scapegoating, and deliberately uncaring statements.

Remember: In shared living situations, eliminating clutter will mean resolving relationship clutter, but you can't force someone to do this with you. All you can do is share your feelings, validate theirs, and ask for change in ways that don't create more emotional clutter.

Getting everyone on track and on the organizing train, and to be the conductor of their own life, takes insight, creative strategy, and know-how. The Clutter Remedy offer the most organized and stress-free way for individuals, families, and businesses to get organized for good.

3

THE CLUTTER
REMEDY STRATEGY

I'm acutely aware that millions of people are keen on getting their space organized. "Getting organized," like any lifestyle change, has become as popular as "losing weight" and "increasing wealth." You can express that you want to get rid of a ton of stuff, resulting in you releasing nothing, or you can be hesitant about releasing anything at all and end up giving away the farm. When you start the organizing and decluttering process, think about the end result: a finely tuned categorized space, where everything you own, within your cabinets, closets, and storage areas, has a specific home and is contained and easily accessible. Using the Clutter Remedy strategy is an easy and empowering way to make good decisions without regret, hesitation, and angst.

You want the stars to align when you're doing this amazingly cleansing project. It is not a laissez-faire type of experience. You don't want the attitude of allowing things to just take their own course. Preparation is key to having it go smoothly, and this chapter describes the concise and well-planned strategy, the specific steps, and the proper organizing tools.

This strategy can be customized for any residential or business areas — whether a bathroom, office, kitchen, bedroom, garage, attic, or basement — as well as adapted to your individual lifestyle. It is hard to imagine that in a short period of time your life will change forever and in such a great way. Through this process, you will learn about yourself as you shape your space to support your life dreams. Once completed, you will never look back, only forward to a new way of living. All of your clutter will turn into beautiful collections, all of your scattered items will be displayed, and you will learn to symbolize everything you own.

SYMBOLIZE COLLECTIONS

Sometimes, for sentimental reasons, you will amass a vast abundance of a certain item — like travel souvenirs, specific themed knickknacks like collections of owls or frogs, books, shoes, toys, and hats — and you can get stuck deciding what to do with them.

If this comes up for you, the strategy I recommend is to symbolize your collection. This can be done for any individual item, but it's particularly helpful for sentimental objects that don't have any use or function. In essence, ask yourself, "What does this object represent to me or in my life?" Then, once you identify what the object or collection represents, ask, "Does that symbol make me happy or sad? Does it inspire me and represent who I am now, or does it make me feel depressed and relate to who I once was?"

Some people have no idea what I mean when I ask them to "symbolize" their stuff. However, all objects have symbolic meaning. What this process does is get you to look beyond the literal, functional purpose of an object and ask what the object means to you, symbolically. Does it represent a certain status or role? Does it embody a certain emotion or value? Symbolizing a collection helps you understand why you started collecting that type of object and why it "spoke" to you in the first place.

For example, Danielle was a divorced empty nester who wanted to declutter and get the cobwebs out of her house and life. To her shock and annoyance, she found she owned twenty empty picture frames. She had bought them intending to create a picture wall of her family, and yet somehow she had never carved out the time. They were nice, useful frames, and I asked Danielle to symbolize them as a collection. She said they meant "family unity." That, obviously, did not represent her life anymore, not after her "bitter divorce" and now that her children were grown and gone. So Danielle kept a few and donated the rest to a college art department. Sometimes there is regret when you address the past, yet that is replaced by the satisfaction of honoring who you are now and of getting and staying organized for good.

For Frances, her collection of sponges symbolized "alone time." Every time she wanted time alone, Frances would give her husband a coupon to go buy more sponges. For Samantha, another client who collected sponges, the sponges meant she was "clean and sanitary, and inviting company over." For these two women, symbolizing the sponges helped them understand that the sponges were not truly an avenue to a more ideal lifestyle. Frances realized that setting aside time for herself to draw and paint without interruption required setting boundaries with her husband. For Samantha, who valued socializing and entertaining, going out to learn ballroom dancing linked her to a new group of friends, and the motivation to clear and clean her home came from the stimulation of friendship.

Miriam collected dolphin-themed objects — including plates, knickknacks, dish towels, trivets, planters, pictures, and mobiles.

They symbolized a connection to her late husband and to all the family, friends, and coworkers who had given her the dolphins over many years. Miriam symbolized each and every object, since most had a different symbolic meaning based on who gave them to her. She realized these objects never helped her reconnect to friends and family or to develop close relationships, which she valued. Some dolphins symbolized nothing at all. Miriam released 70 percent of the dolphin objects, and she started to email and call her family and friends and update them on her life. Instead of reminiscing through her dolphins, she renewed her relationships with people who loved her unconditionally.

Mel called for help unpacking a new home after his wife died. He had so much breathtakingly beautiful crystal and expensive, splendid objects. This included over eighty tea cup sets that Mel and his wife had collected together over the course of forty-eight years. The tea cups meant happier days for Mel and symbolized his love for his wife. Mel explained, "I know where every tea cup came from, and it helps me with remembering my wife and our time together." Mel chose to keep all the tea cups. Mel and I found some large antique lighted cabinets to display many of them, and more were sprinkled around the house. Those he didn't display were carefully wrapped and stored in plastic bins in the garage. When I asked Mel what he would do with all the cups if he met someone new, he replied, "I'll wait to see if my new 'flame' will like the cups as much as my late wife and I did."

Symbolizing your belongings is a great way to evaluate if what you've collected is actually helping you achieve what you want out of life and to understand what they represent to you on a deeper level. For Karen, her collection of toothbrushes symbolized "nicer teeth" and being a "polished" type of person; for Mary, who was lonely and never had guests, tons of serving platters meant company; for Andrew, his over three hundred books represented being smart and his aspiration to become number one at his company; for Randall, an older gentleman with crippling arthritis, his tools meant handiness and being competent; for Nick and Sandy, their antiques symbolized having wealth and great taste. But when I asked each and every one of those clients whether any of the objects in their collections had ever helped them achieve their actual desires, the answer was the same: No.

When you keep collections displayed and set up properly, and in a polished and pleasing way, protected and admired within beautiful cabinets or on shelves, collections are amazing. Rare stuff, fabulous and marvelous objects of pure beauty, exquisite and aesthetic things — these are awesome to collect. But when precious things are neglected, could it mean you are symbolically neglecting yourself, your goals, and the things you truly value in life? Notice if objects you have forgotten about or lost in drawers symbolize a lost or forgotten part of yourself. Remember, your inner self has all the answers, and the Clutter Remedy strategy will help you recognize what's truly meant to stay in your life.

PREPARE TO BECOME PERPETUALLY ORGANIZED

I know you want to be organized and you are getting the closest you have come to creating a clutter-free, satisfying space, aligned with all that you cherish in life. I also know you don't wake up in the morning and think, "I'm going to make a big mess today!" I know you don't say, "I love it when my things are all over the place." Yet I'm certain you are not jumping up and down saying, "Oh goody, I'm so happy I get to clean out the pantry, the garage, and the attic today," either. You crave an organized inner self and space yet loathe or can't figure out the process of getting either organized. The desire to be organized is in all of us, but the more you want to achieve it, the more it creates a state of what I call "perpetual disorganization." Perpetual disorganization means a lack of understanding about what you truly value in life, a lack of optimal communication skills and relationships, and a lack of an organized inner self and space. Perpetual disorganization is the state of being chronically messy, without a strategy to store items, resulting in a lack of ease in finding important things. It leaves one feeling frustrated and in the state of being "perpetually disorganized." Another aspect of perpetual disorganization is alternating from disorganized to organized and then back to disorganized on a regular basis. You straighten up and get organized, but two days, two weeks, or two months later there is a big mess again with clumps of clutter everywhere. It is a repetitive, tiring cycle.

If you have been floundering around the organizational process for a while now and wondering where and how to start, well, the clock on organizing starts when you are ready to understand the difference between being perpetually disorganized versus perpetually organized. An organized space does not make your life tick, although you may be able to move about more freely. Learning how to brilliantly extinguish clutter and manifest a clear, functional, and vibrant space helps you understand that organizing and decluttering is about creating an environment that you are pleased with, that creates energy for you, rather than stagnancy. Getting organized involves knowing what to do with every single tangible thing about you, your life, and what you own, while creating a perpetually organized and welcoming space.

The opposite state of having perpetual disorganization is "perpetual organization." Perpetual organization is having an understanding of what you truly value in life, having optimal communication skills and relationships, and having an organized inner self and space. It is the state of being perpetually organized, with a system to store items, resulting in an ease in finding important items. It leaves one feeling settled and calm. Another aspect of perpetual organization is remaining organized long-term.

Being perpetually organized is living without clutter, and

keeping everything that you want in your life, with easy access to it all. Becoming perpetually organized is not only about being "neat" and "tidy." Perpetual organization is about having everything you own categorized, into finely tuned categories, contained in a proper way, and placed in an appropriate home. Getting motivated to transition from a perpetually disorganized lifestyle to an organized one is a life-altering moment and easily managed with the Clutter Remedy strategy. One of the best results of becoming perpetually organized is living an exquisite and breezy clutter-free life.

Preparing to get your digs ready for year-round success is optimal when the weather is picture-perfect and your energy is high. You will be super busy visualizing, planning, shopping, gathering your organizing tools, and delving in to create your clutter-free dream space.

VISUALIZE AND ASSESS YOUR SPACE

When you're ready to begin your organized lifestyle, start by naming your core values and visualizing your life goals, per the advice in chapter 1. Then, before starting any of the physical aspects of getting organized, do another contemplative exercise. Visualize your space as it currently is. Visualize every aspect of your space in its current cluttered state. Take a few deep breaths and feel the emotions associated with your current space. Now open your eyes and sit for a few minutes with those feelings.

Next, close your eyes and visualize your space the way you want it to be. Visualize everything in order and categorized. Make it the most beautiful and vibrant space you can imagine. Take a few deep breaths and feel the emotions associated with your newly developed space. Now open your eyes and sit for a few minutes with the feelings associated with your new space.

Remember and return to these visualizations as you work, since they will help guide you as you plan, declutter, and organize.

Next, on a practical level, assess the space and all the stuff in it. Look through every room, and look into every nook and cranny. Look at the entire space regardless of what room or rooms you're working on. Look in every cabinet, drawer, and closet; look under and behind every piece of furniture, including your bed. Take notes as you go, especially of any and every empty or underutilized space that could be used as storage space.

Assess how your furniture is placed. Doing a furniture placement assessment is important for identifying how to arrange your space better, for both livability and extra storage. Moving furniture will often create more wall space, which will create more places to put armoires, shelves, and cabinets to store and display the items you choose to keep and to prevent recluttering.

Measure your wall space and your furniture, and sketch out or visualize a new design for the space that will accommodate where any extra storage and containment pieces will go. See how furniture pieces will fit. Even an inch or two in measuring where pieces will go makes a difference. Designing the optimal space means creating good energy and flow (see chapter 6 for more on this).

Then, make sure to take "before" pictures of your entire space.

ASSESS AND PLAN
FOR SUFFICIENT STORAGE

Creating adequate, accessible "storing areas" is a major key to becoming perpetually organized. Evaluate the best ways to store regularly used items within every room, and strategize where you will move and put seldom-used items or things to be stored out of the immediate living space. While you can't make every decision ahead, it's important to create a general storage plan first, before decluttering, since proper storage can involve buying new furniture, storage bins, and other containment devices, or building useful storage.

To plan well, evaluate both what you anticipate keeping and how often you use those items, then consider the best places and ways to store those things, given the configuration of each space. What this means will vary, and most plans will be adjusted as you go through the decluttering process. I like to look at all existing storing areas together, to get the whole picture of what's available, considering attics, basements, garages, closets, cabinets, shelves, and drawers. Consider the best places to put things you use daily, weekly, monthly, occasionally, or seasonally. The things you use the most will stay closest, and the things you use the least will be put farther away. During the categorizing process, you will find similar items scattered among various places, and you will start to gather them into broad categories. Most existing storing areas typically hold a jumbled mess of uncategorized objects, which is a major cause of perpetual disorganization. Instead, you will place all items into defined categories and create a well-thought-out plan so that every categorized item has a place, and all storing areas are identified and used properly. Many times, rooms have ample space for storage, but they are simply poorly and haphazardly arranged and disorganized. Many times, large storing areas are underutilized and not taken advantage of, and they have lots of empty, available space.

When rooms lack adequate storing areas, get creative. It's optimal for regularly used items to be stored in or nearest to the room where they are used most often. For example, in a small kitchen, storage for food and cooking utensils will be prioritized, while less-used items (like bulk goods, entertainment pieces, mixers, large pots and pans) will be stored outside the kitchen. Going through the process of finding a home for everything you want to keep helps you become more thoughtful about where and how to store certain things, and to do so more efficiently and purposefully than you have in the past. For instance, you can create a shoe closet near the entrance of your home, or in the garage, so you

don't bring shoes into the living or bedroom areas. You can dedicate a closet in a guest room for all of your coats and not mix them
in your bedroom or hall closets. Having a seasonal gift and wrapping closet will be delightful when you have lots of celebrations
that you attend. Consider what you will build or buy to create
more useful space. Could you build shelves into a closet? Or re
place unwieldy furniture with new pieces that have more storage
or provide the kind of storage that will be useful?

Ultimately, you want the storing areas to be purposeful, easy
to access, and categorized by how often you use things. When
you start behaving like a treasure hunter, rummaging around and
looking all over the place for what you want, it creates angst and
futility. You don't want to be tearing up a closet or getting out a
treasure map to find your stuff, so before deciding what to keep,
it's also important to anticipate where everything will go. Don't
start putting anything away, though, until all items are categorized, gone through, fine-tuned, and contained.

OTHER PEOPLE'S STUFF
AND SHARED SPACE

A big question or concern I hear often is "What do I do with
other people's stuff?" Many times I come into a shared living situation, and everyone is pointing fingers at everyone else's mess,
while conveniently overlooking their own mess. Pointing fingers
doesn't clear up a mess. Helping hands do.

Every situation is different. It could be an empty nester whose
space is cluttered with their adult child's memorabilia, which they
left behind long ago. It could be a business or office shared by two
or more people with different visions and expectations. It could
be couples or roommates wanting to simplify and divide their
space so they can combine two households in a way that works
best for all. It could be a family with different-age children, including some so young their job title could be "toy distributor."

It could be that you have ended up with inherited stuff that you don't know what to do with. Figuring out stuff, anybody's stuff, is easy with the Clutter Remedy strategy, even when you're the only one wanting to get organized.

When family members or roommates use shared living spaces, or use shared storing areas, you want them to be responsible for going through their own items using the Clutter Remedy strategy. Begin with your own stuff and become a model for being organized. Generally, everyone under the same roof will join in, but if not, setting boundaries and using the Assertive Language and Validation Tool (see pages 42–45) will be helpful. Obviously, if someone you're living or working with does not want to participate and declutter with you, you do not want to violate them by throwing out their belongings. Be respectful and share the principles of the Clutter Remedy strategy, which is not about getting rid of stuff. The strategy is about categorizing everything, fine-tuning those categories, and finding the appropriate home for everything that's owned. Give others a time period and opportunities to manage their things in a shared space first, and then set up guidelines for how you want the home to be long-term, starting by sharing your feelings and validating the feelings of others (see "Resolving Conflicts: Assertive Language and Validation Tool," pages 42–45). When kids or other family members have moved out, set a time limit for them to claim their belongings before you reclaim "their" space as "your" space. Other people's stuff holds energy and can become a nuisance to your life goals, so having conversations and working through clutter conflict will be worth it, to get your space sorted out once and for all.

Conflicts over OPS and Decluttering Relationships

Where it gets tricky is when one person feels encroached upon by other people's stuff, or what I call "OPS," and when the other person feels unfairly accused and judged or doesn't agree that there's a problem. Complaints range from how much stuff someone else has to what they're holding on to or collecting to simply the desire for more darn space. Sometimes the person complaining is playing an equal part in the mess, and sometimes they are indeed suffering beneath the weight of someone else's jumble. Sometimes all parties appeal to me as if I were the clutter complaint department or the clutter judge, but I remind them that decluttering is not a competition and clutter is not a crime. Rather, it's a shared challenge, and to deal with it successfully, everyone who lives under the same roof becomes responsible for organizing their own self and space and staying clutter-free.

Remember: Outer space is a reflection of inner space. The same is true in a shared living situation. External clutter reflects both personal and interpersonal dynamics within relationships. In other words, clutter can be an expression of a dysfunctional relationship, and healing that dysfunction will be crucial to fixing the clutter. Each person in a shared living situation will want to clarify their own inner emotional blocks as well as recognize how their stuff and their habits impact others. One person will feel stifled and believe the stuff is taking over, while the other person will feel enthralled by being king of their heap. In a relationship, arguments and not seeing eye to eye about OPS can become a huge power and control struggle if you are not careful. It can break apart relationships and marriages. Housekeeping is one of the top five arguments people living under one roof have. When everyone's feelings get hurt, arguments over who's more at fault undermine finding solutions for an organized space.

When people in relationships go through the decluttering process, they sometimes gain unexpected clarity about their relationship, in the same way that people gain clarity about their life goals, and this can lead them to make significant changes in their relationship. I've seen couples grow closer and heal through this process, and I've seen people split up upon realizing that their clutter is signaling deeper, hidden challenges in their relationship. I've also seen situations where two or more people were equal partners in cluttering. They supported one another's habits and were comfortable with them, until the situation became truly unworkable: They found they couldn't move or walk about freely, or they began receiving complaints from neighbors and landlords. You could say, these people happily shared the same clutter challenge, which led to not being able to function at all.

Kyle complained about his wife, Margo, carting excessive amounts of stuff into their house on a regular basis, until he couldn't sit on the couch or safely make his way down hallways. He shared his feelings of discomfort and despair with Margo, and he set some boundaries, but no matter how much he told her that the clutter bothered him, she would not stop accumulating. Kyle even threatened to leave Margo, but she still would not stop collecting, accumulating, and dropping stuff everywhere. Kyle loved so many things about his wife, but he felt disrespected and even unloved. Ultimately, Kyle did move out as a trial separation, to see if it would motivate Margo to agree to an organizing and decluttering project. Kyle explained to Margo that nothing she collected had to go, and everything would be categorized, organized, and have a home. This was out of the question for Margo, and she simply ignored his pleas for clear space. Eventually, Kyle came to realize that Margo was using stuff as a boundary to keep him out, which was heartbreaking. After a few years of waiting and urging Margo to change, Kyle filed for divorce. In a literal way, Margo wouldn't make room for him, and Kyle realized that he wanted to move forward and find someone who would.

Linda and Rob were a senior couple living in a two-bedroom condominium that was so cluttered I could only take a few steps into the entrance. Carefully navigating the slightest of paths, I peered into the living room, which had mounds up to the ceiling divided by trenches for pathways. Standing in the midst of this momentous mass were Linda and Rob, looking like they were floating in papers and magazines and random stuff. Linda came crawling toward me over packed molehills of stuff as if it were perfectly normal, then she led me carefully down a short hallway to her bedroom, which was blocked by a nine-by-sixteen-foot hill of clothing, books, purses, shoes, papers, glassware, boxes, blankets, towels, sheets, and anything else you could imagine. When Linda asked if I wanted to climb over the hill and enter her room, I said no as respectfully as I could. It was too dangerous, and I was not wearing the appropriate gear for that environment. She agreed.

Then Linda told me their stories. For the past twenty years, Linda had used collecting as a coping strategy for her painful memories of child abuse, and her husband, Rob, was a war veteran who also coped with his own painful memories by collecting. They had been, Linda said, "quite comfortable" with their situation until an upcoming building inspection had them worried about getting caught and fined. They came up with the idea of having me come out and temporarily remove everything and bring it back after the inspection. When I realized they had no intention of creating a long-term clutter-free solution, I suggested a less-expensive option, which was to use movers. Ultimately, they did not go through with the organizing process. Given the sheer volume of stuff, they decided it would be too painful, physically, mentally, and emotionally. So they hired movers to take their stuff to a storage unit, and when the building inspections were completed, they brought all the stuff back. Obviously, this is an extreme case of overcollecting and overaccumulation. But Linda and Rob chose this lifestyle freely, and they chose it together, and after considering all my suggestions and warnings, they decided to continue as they were.

When people hire me, it isn't my place to condemn their clutter. When people are genuinely comfortable with their situation, even when it's extreme, I am not the conductor of their life; they are. However, most often, people are fed up with their mess, and they don't know how to get out of it. As with Linda and Rob, a couple or family can live and cope with clutter for decades until they are threatened with eviction by a family member or a landlord. In these situations — even when the mess is cleared up, and everything has been categorized, contained, and put away — the possibility of relapsing back into clutter is high unless the people involved do the inner emotional healing work that led to the mess in the first place.

Reliable and experienced professional organizers are not housekeepers or personal assistants. I always look at the whole picture and figure out an individualized system to support an organized life. I recognize if someone can handle the process and, if not, there is nothing anyone can do, except give advice, be concerned, and hope that someday there will be a clearing and healing process. Even city officials, police, and the fire department are not allowed to tell someone how to live.

When you're ready to clean house, and after you've assessed your space and your available storage, it is time to gather your organizing supplies and tools, get physical, and put on your organizing gloves.

BUDGET AND SHOP

You can spend as much or as little on this process as you want. However, the nature of your budget certainly influences your options. As I discuss in chapter 6, some people include this process as part of a larger remodeling that includes new paint, new furniture, new flooring, and other design options. When you don't have too much money to spend, work with the space and the furniture you have. Both options can be successful. The important thing is to have enough places, furniture, and storing pieces to put all your belongings and create an ideal space.

I had one client who became very indignant when I suggested buying some new furniture so he could put away all of the items he wanted to keep. I replied, "Where do you want to put all of your stuff, in midair?" No matter what size your budget, you want to be realistic about your storage space. Sometimes, to solve a critical storage challenge, it's a worthwhile long-term investment to buy the exact type of furniture that will hold all your belongings successfully, whether that's an armoire, a free-standing cabinet, new bookshelves, or a dresser. In essence, money will buy you space.

Another purchase that is crucial to the Clutter Remedy strategy includes a range of clear storage bins, decorative containers, totes, tubs, boxes, baskets, and organizers. As I explain below, items in every type of category will be contained together. Putting your finely tuned categories into the perfectly sized bins, baskets, containers, and drawer organizers to keep things separate is the secret to perpetual organization. Ahead of time, strategize the number and type of bins you think will hold all the items coming out of the space. You will simply guesstimate how many containment-type solutions will be helpful for the categorizing process and for placing things back into your space and storage areas. Buy as much as you can afford, while using anything that you currently own that will be helpful to the process. It never hurts to have extra bins available, since you can always return or sell those you don't use. Purchase a variety of sizes, from small to very large. For items you will store long-term in garages, attics, basements, closets, or storage units, I prefer bins with locking handles, since they stack well and the lids won't pop open easily.

To save money, get creative about furniture you already own. Reinvent or repurpose credenzas, sideboards, and buffet tables as storage for toys and crafts. I once turned an old entertainment center armoire into a pantry by building shelving inside it. No one knows what is behind closed doors. Shop at thrift or secondhand stores for gently used items and online resale venues to find bargains and even free items. Planning and shopping ahead, especially when existing storage space is tight, is incredibly helpful during the process of putting your space back together after decluttering. Remember: This strategy is not about "getting rid of stuff," although you most likely will do that in the process. It's about accommodating and organizing all the things you love and want to keep, without regret and angst.

MAKE A PLAN:
TIME, TOOLS, AND SUPPORT

Planning is essential for having the process go smoothly. Once you've mapped out and visualized how you will change your space, create a concise, well-planned strategy for the hands-on work of decluttering and organizing.

How long will the process take? Less time than you think. The strategy is designed to be completed within a fairly short period of time, since that's most effective and efficient. I recommend setting aside at least two to three consecutive days and planning to spend from four to six uninterrupted hours each day focused on decluttering and organizing. Single rooms can be completed in a day, while homes that are filled to the brim will obviously take longer.

What I don't recommend is working an hour here and an hour there, over the course of weeks or months, being inconsistent, or doing it in the midst of a busy schedule. It will be too difficult to jump in and out of the process, and this will create frustration. The process happens twice as fast when it is done succinctly in a shorter period of time — especially when you allow enough time to process your belongings without taking them in and out of your space and categorizing area.

There is nothing worse than spending most of the day

clearing out a garage and only getting halfway through categorizing before you run out of sunlight, leaving you to haul everything unfinished back into the garage and, of course, haul it back out the next day to continue where you left off. When you have a tremendous amount of stuff to categorize and fine-tune, avoid that back-and-forth movement by removing only half the contents from the space. The next day, do the other half, and then combine like categories from both days together at the end.

While clearing and categorizing, you don't want to be disturbed or regularly interrupted. Set aside enough time so that you work safely and with your full attention on the project.

Your stamina will also determine how efficient and successful you are. Get adequate sleep beforehand, eat well, hydrate regularly, and stretch. Have water and snacks with you at all times. Decluttering is like doing aerobics, no kidding. At any point, when you become tired, run down, hungry, weary, or bleary-eyed, take a break. No one makes good decisions when they're exhausted or worn-out (for more advice on taking care of yourself during this process, see chapter 7).

Using a team of organizers, I have organized the most extreme cases in two to three days. I suggest getting some supportive and strong people to help you when you're in this type of situation. Of course, you can do a project on your own; don't let me give you the wrong idea, but it will take much more time, and a lot of the work is physical and includes climbing ladders, moving furniture, and lifting heavy bins of stuff.

Asking for help is especially important when lifting, moving, or building heavy racks, or when you are climbing up ladders to reach high places. Ask honest, nonjudgmental, easygoing, and supportive friends and family. If you prefer, hire movers, which is not a sign of weakness. Even if it's only for a few items, get the extra hands to make the decluttering process delightful instead of backbreaking. You want your decluttering project to be safe and sound, and you don't want to hurt yourself. Also, supportive helpers, whether friends, family, or neighborhood kids, will make the process more fun, and they can offer emotional support, too. When it is absolutely physically impossible to do anything at all on your own, find someone local to help who is familiar with the Clutter Remedy strategy.

Gather Helpful Organizing Tools

As I say above, assess what you anticipate storing and containing, and buy ahead of time whatever bins, containers, and furniture will be useful during your project.

It's also helpful to gather a range of supplies and tools. You don't want to be stymied because you lack a box cutter or run out of trash bags. Below is a list of useful things to have on hand. Ideally, you already possess or can borrow most of them, but if not, gather or buy the proper tools and gear prior to starting.

- Dust masks
- Safety glasses
- Hat for outdoors
- Tape measure
- Scissors/box cutters
- Dolly
- Permanent markers
- Camera
- Cardboard boxes (recycled) and large white bags for donations
- Large black trash bags for rubbish

- Gloves
- Ladders and step stools
- Pen and paper
- A fully charged phone
- Paper towels
- Cleansers
- Vacuum
- Duster/rags
- Broom and dust pan
- Tape
- Basic toolbox
- A lock box for valuables
- A dumpster

ARRANGE THE CATEGORIZING AREA
AND EMPTY THE SPACE

The decluttering and categorizing process requires some room. It starts by emptying the space you're organizing and dividing items into categories, so strategize and arrange the area you choose to work in. Determine where the "categorizing area" will be and where you will put items for donation and items to be trashed. If you will be throwing out a lot of trash, consider renting a dumpster. Trash is considered to be anything that cannot be donated, gifted, or sold or that you will want sent to a toxic and e-waste facility in your area. Please be responsible when disposing of chemicals, old paint, and electronics.

I recommend categorizing in the largest clear area you have, like a nearly empty garage or a covered patio. If the weather is nice, working outside in the front or backyard also works well (but wear a hat and use sunscreen). When decluttering in a smaller space, like a tiny apartment or studio, or within a single office, do the best you can. If possible, make use of an adjacent hallway or room, and clear as wide an area as you can by moving furniture back and clearing all counters and furniture to make room for empty categorizing bins. When it is a very tight space, clear and categorize objects from sections of the room in stages.

In the "categorizing area," set up rows of empty bins, one for each of the broad categories you create (see pages 67–69). Line up the bins in straight rows, with adequate aisles and plenty of space in between. The bins for some categories will fill up quickly, and some categories will take two or even three bins to hold everything, so leave room for categories to expand as you work. You won't know exactly how many bins you will use until everything is removed from your space, and every single thing is categorized.

Safety always comes first. Keep pathways clear. When carrying items out to the categorizing area, make sure not to step over things. Wear a protective mask, gloves, and eye protection when dealing with dust and debris. My favorite thing to call out during this process is "Clear the path."

Take Out the Trash and Make Donations or Sell Your Stuff

In your categorizing area, set aside a space for items to be thrown away and another space for items to be donated or given to others. Place items to be thrown away immediately into large black trash bags, and place items for donations in white trash bags or old cardboard boxes. As these fill up, take them immediately to the curb. Have one area for trash and another designated area for the donations.

When you have a lot of trash, schedule a special pickup with your town, or rent a dumpster. In addition, get help moving heavy items or items for disposal and recycling, like old refrigerators, microwaves, electronics, old sports equipment, and broken or rusted items.

If you anticipate having a lot of items for donation, call ahead and coordinate a pickup for those items with a local charity. Ideally, schedule them to be picked up on the same day you are clearing out your space. Similarly, if you want to give items to friends and family, confirm that they want those items, and have them take or pick up these gifts as soon as possible, ideally the same day. Avoid storing things you plan to part with for any length of time, since this will slow down the process of setting up your new space. If you will be selling items, do it ahead of time. When things don't sell, and they will not be useful or purposeful, consider donating them.

Name Categories

Part of arranging the categorizing area is naming categories. That is, in broad terms, consider the types of items that belong together, based on what's in the room you will be emptying out.

In a bedroom, for example, some categories will be shoes, pants, linens, jewelry, and photos. Each of these categories will have its own labeled bin.

This is the start of your organizing process, one that will become increasingly fine-tuned as you go. Broad categorizing of everything you own, prior to deciding what you will keep, decreases the stress of decluttering by a hundred notches.

In addition, I recommend making large signs with the name of each category on thick paper and placing them inside the clear storage bins, facing outward. This labeling system helps you sort as you go, and many times, these labels can be used for the bins you decide to store. After categories start to fill up and firm up, the signs become obsolete, since the categories will become obvious.

It doesn't matter what comes out while clearing, and this is not the time to make decisions about what to keep, since that will slow you down. Categorizing does not involve pondering over your stuff. It is not about choosing what to keep or reminiscing. Categorizing is only about gathering and distinguishing what you have into broad categories. Optimally, it's a quick and fast process, once you get the hang of it.

As an example, here is a list of possible broad categories you will start to form:

Sample List of Broad Categories

- Personal items (keys, credit cards, glasses, medications, etc.)
- Bathroom items
- Kitchen items
- Entertaining
- Décor (artwork, lamps, knickknacks, baskets, etc.)
- Phone accessories
- Cords
- Utility (lightbulbs, tools, laundry supplies, etc.)
- Clothing
- Clothing accessories (belts, ties, scarves, hats, etc.)
- Shoes

- Purses
- Jewelry
- Sporting equipment
- Paint
- Cleaning supplies
- Books
- Musical instruments
- Files
- Magazines/newspapers
- Paper
- Office supplies
- Photos
- Toys
- Craft/hobby supplies
- Memorabilia
- Gifts
- Games
- Tools
- Luggage
- Pet supplies
- Small electronics
- Shopping bags (paper and plastic bags)
- Totes
- Linens (sheets, towels, blankets, etc.)
- Food
- Gardening supplies
- Money
- Umbrellas

Empty the Space

Empty out all the items from the space you are decluttering, assign them a category, and place them in a bin. As you go, you will create new categories for items that don't fit already-established categories. That's fine; simply create a new category and assign it a bin.

With a few exceptions that I explain below, the goal is to remove every single thing from every shelf, storage area, drawer, cabinet, and closet. Remove everything from under the beds or that's stored within furniture. Empty every nook and cranny. Open and empty out every box, bag, and filled container, and sort all the loose items into category bins. Don't assume that a box or bag labeled "holiday decorations" contains only decorations. You will be surprised to find dental products, old linens, and who knows what in such boxes or bags. Leave no clutter unturned.

An exception to this rule is any bag that you know you will keep and that holds a single category of items, like a medical kit or a golf bag. Keep these types of contained items intact.

Move at a comfortable pace, and keep your path clear at all times. Watch your step when filling the bins. For this part of the process, stay focused on emptying all of the contents of your entire space and separating items into broad categories. Remember, don't get caught up evaluating any items or deciding what you will keep during this part of the strategy.

When space is tight in the categorizing area, empty rooms and process items in stages. After everything has been removed from the main space, items in the kitchen, bathroom, and office cabinets can be pulled out and categorized separately. However, if, say, you have kitchen items stored all over the house, you will want to gather and divide all the kitchen items into categories before moving on to the next step, which is deciding what to keep.

That said, here are some types of things you do not want to remove from the space or place in a categorizing bin.

- Valuables/breakables: keep them inside in a safe place
- Heavy furniture or rugs
- Heavy electronics, computers, and printers that you are keeping
- Artwork on the walls that you are keeping
- Hanging clothes and other hanging items in closets: once the rest of the space is organized, you can categorize and process hanging items directly from within the closets (see "A Restful Bedroom," page 81)

DECIDE WHAT TO KEEP: FOUR CLEAR AND CONCISE CRITERIA

Once your space is empty and all items are gathered into broad categories, it's time to declutter. Evaluate each thing you own and decide whether to keep it, donate it, gift it, sell it, recycle it, throw it away, or take it to a toxic/e-waste disposal center.

Here is your first step to decluttering your life. Focusing on one bin and category at a time, pull out each item and ask the following four Clear and Concise Criteria questions:

- Is it useful?
- Does it serve a purpose?
- Is it sentimental?
- Do I love it?

Asking these four Clear and Concise Criteria questions will transform how you perceive everything you own. These criteria make every single thing you own come alive with clarity. The criteria will turn doubt or curiosity into certainty. The questions will help you determine quickly what to keep or release with care and consideration and — most importantly — easily and without regret. You will become a master rather than a slave to the utter nonsense of clutter. Living clearly, clutter-free, making sense of all that you own, and knowing how and where to put everything will make you a better organizer for the rest of your life. The criteria help you identify what matters to you, what fits into your current lifestyle, and how often you use things.

Do you even know what you use? Do you use an item daily, weekly, monthly, or twice a year? Even if an item is used only seasonally or occasionally, like your turkey platter, it's to be kept. I call it a "keep." You're not going to get rid of that. Do you know the things that serve a purpose? As long as things serve a purpose, they are "keeps." They can be rarely used tools, like the key to the fireplace, or backup items that you may never use, like an extra key to the car, safe, or community pool — as long as they serve a purpose they are keeps, and you're not going to get rid of those items. How about sentimental items? Pictures, memorabilia, recordings, kids' artwork, old diaries, journals, your yearbooks. Sentimental items are "keeps." Your mementos certainly are keepers, even when they're hidden in a box. And you clearly know what you love. Jewelry, books, collectibles, artwork, dishes, décor, furniture, knickknacks, clothes, bags, shoes, bedding, hair supplies, and beauty items are things you love to have around you. These items make you feel calm, happy, or accomplished. You will want to keep them. They're not going anywhere.

Here are some other ideas to think about for your second step and to continue getting decluttered. Think about all of the stuff that you decided to keep for a minute. Do you know what you treasure the most, out of everything, and what you don't treasure at all? Do you know what makes you warm and fuzzy or frosty frozen? Do you know which things you want to keep or chuck, to store or display? Do you want to stop shoving and hiding your clutter trappings to get them out of sight? Did you know, before categorizing, where all your "good" possessions were stashed, or were you always looking around for your valuables? Knowing the difference between the accumulation of junk and things you treasure helps you protect what you love in the future.

Clutter can turn into "loved stuff," but until processed into viable finely tuned categories, clutter will remain clutter. Clutter did not magically appear. It was not dropped into your life and space by a clutter fairy or blown in from a wild wind tunnel. You either brought it in yourself or you accepted it from the outside world. Once the clutter arrives, it becomes all the material objects in your life that are out of order, spread out, and unloved. Every material thing you own is there for one reason or another. Not one thing in your space walked in by itself and decided it would be loved or neglected. However, remember, stuff is not the big stuff in life: The big stuff in life is the people you love and who love you, along with your health, happiness, and living an accomplished and finely tuned ideal lifestyle.

FINE-TUNE CATEGORIES
AND ORGANIZE YOUR SPACE

Now you have come to the crux of the Clutter Remedy strategy, the crème de la crème of organizing. Once your space is empty and you've decided what to keep, "fine-tune" your categories and find homes for every object. This is where you reorganize your space and store your things so that they inspire and support your life. Through fine-tuning and storing, you create perpetual organization. Fine-tuning everything you keep helps you become more thoughtful about the way you live, and proper storage makes everything you own easy to find and access. Ideally, the process will help you become more efficient and purposeful in everything you do.

Fine-Tune Your Categories

Once a broad category bin contains only items you want to keep, fine-tune the items into subcategories, matching each and every particular type of object together. This is a very therapeutic part of the process and the most important part of the strategy for long-term, perpetual organization. For example, within the electronics category, computer cords, phone cords, mice, and keyboards are all made into separate categories from gaming consoles and controllers. To be clear, this means all mice with mice, keyboards with keyboards, phone cords with phone cords, and computer cords with computer cords. Within the office supply category, make separate subcategories for every distinct item: staples, paper clips, pushpins, scissors, pens, journals, and notepads. Keep subcategorizing until every object is with every like object.

A single broad category will often contain dozens of subcategories. As when creating the broad categories, you can name or arrange your subcategories in whatever way suits you, but be very specific and exact. Don't contain a mixture of subcategories together. In other words, no "mixed venues," as I call it. This means gathering every rubber band you own with every other rubber band; every hair clip with other hair clips; every candle with every other candle; every lightbulb with every other lightbulb. When even subcategories have distinctions, further distinguish them by type and size. For instance, books: Place all sports books together, design with design, fiction with fiction, and poetry with poetry. Organize different types of shoes with like kinds. Keep athletic shoes with every other athletic shoe, slippers with slippers, dress shoes with dress shoes. Do the same with types of socks, pants, shirts, and other categories. This process will seem tedious, but it's essential to fine-tune to remain permanently organized.

Contain All Like Items

The next essential step of the Clutter Remedy strategy is to *contain* all finely tuned categories. Each finely tuned category will go in some form of containment. What containment will work best depends on the size of the category itself and how and where it will be displayed or stored. You want the containment to perfectly fit whatever it holds and not be half empty or overflowing.

Types of containment include zipped bags, clear bins, decorative baskets, boxes, totes, tubs, and drawer inserts. For storage in the garage or inside cabinets, clear bins are optimal. Decorative or fabric-covered bins or boxes are optimal for items that will be seen or displayed on shelves and that you want close at hand. Purchase designer bins or ones that are more decorative and yet purely functional; choosing options that are aesthetically pleasing will make you happier. Storage can also be unusual or creative: While special storage containers are made to hold wrapping paper, you can create a wrapping station out of a dresser with drawers that perfectly fit your paper; that works, too. When you are looking through all your wares during the process, keep any totes, bins, baskets, large bowls, or anything that could hold a category nicely.

Containing each fine-tuned category keeps each and every category separated for good. If you are keeping four hairbrushes, contain them together in a correctly sized space, whether it is a bin, basket, or drawer, and don't mix them with combs. Combs would be contained separately. If you have only a few barrettes, place them in a zipped plastic bag or a pouch, so they do not mix with rubber bands or float free in a drawer. Categorizing and containing every single thing you own is how you stay organized long-term.

Otherwise, you will experience the "schmoosh" effect. When you put things on shelves that are not contained — whether it is cans of soup, pasta, and cookies on a pantry shelf — they will eventually meld and "schmoosh" together. Same when socks, underwear, and T-shirts are mashed in the same drawer: They will meld and "schmoosh," and clutter chaos will return. Things can go inside a zipped plastic bag (for small loose items), a drawer insert, a bin, a box, or any type of receptacle. Even two related but different items will be contained separately. For instance, nail scissors and nail files are not stored together in one type of containment, nor are pens with pencils. Unless each and every item is separated by some barrier, you are not creating a "fine-tuned" system. Several fine-tuned subcategories can be placed together in a larger container as long as each category also has its own containment. For instance, when nail files, nail scissors, polish, and clippers are each contained separately, then they can be put together into a single bin. Every single solitary category, no matter how tiny or large, will remain separated for life. Obviously valuable and breakable decorative items will not be contained, and they will go directly on shelves, mantels, and tabletops, but being obsessive about containing all other items ensures a decluttered life.

Next in the Clutter Remedy strategy you will find a home for all your belongings. Be aware, prior to putting things away, that I have four specific rules for keeping an organized space organized for good.

Four Rules for an Organized Space

Similar to the four Clear and Concise Criteria for evaluating your things, I have Four Rules to check off regularly, to keep your space perpetually organized. That's it, four rules. Follow them, and you will always stay organized.

1. No things or piles on the floor. Check.
2. No things or piles on surfaces, except for regular, high-use items. Check.
3. All things fine-tuned and contained. Check.
4. Everything you own put away in a convenient home. Check.

There is one exception to rule number two: When there are certain regular, high-use items that you want readily available, you can keep them on a surface when they fit the purpose of the space. For instance, you want your coffee pot on the kitchen counter; cologne and perfume and your electric toothbrush on your bathroom counter; certain cooking utensils in a lovely container near your stove; and a stapler on your desk. Also, you can place décor items directly onto surfaces. Decorative items can be placed on shelves, mantels, tables, and wherever they are best displayed. However, be vigilant not to let loose items creep onto counters and surfaces simply because you aren't *willing* yourself to put them away.

Find a Home for Every Object

The final step to the Clutter Remedy strategy is finding a home for every object and fine-tuned contained category, based on where and how often you use it. Where categories end up is like putting together a puzzle. Fitting categories nicely and purposefully back into your space creates a harmonious picture, so that your outer space will look fabulous no matter what you are keeping.

Where things will fit best depends on the room, how you use the object, the size of the object or category, the type of containment, and most of all how often you use it. At this point, refer to the space design plan you developed during the initial assessment of your space. This is the moment to rearrange furniture, shelves, and cabinets and to place any found, bought, or built furniture or storage containers into your space.

Of course, you will want to tweak the plan depending on how much or little you have kept. Evaluate what you have kept, and as new ideas spring forth from the process itself, be creative in setting up the best space possible. Remember, a space with good energy and flow is optimal. Once your space is cleared, you have a clean slate and are ready to set up your ideal space. Analyze your space to see how to make it more functional prior to putting things away. When you find during the process of putting things away that you are still short on storage space, or things are in disrepair, be creative and find cabinets and shelves to hold your belongings. When you become inspired to do a more involved remodel to reinvigorate your space, one that requires contractors, see chapter 6. For reinvigorating your space, hire a contractor *after* decluttering. Getting your space custom-designed around what you will be keeping is a smart way to stay clutter-free.

As you consider the appropriate place for your categorized and contained items, think of the container as the "home" for your stuff, and the space as the property or the "lot" for each contained "home." Think of every desk, kitchen cabinet, bathroom drawer, or dresser as real estate for a neighborhood of things, each living in its own house. Deciding where you will store each category involves determining where it makes the most sense in your everyday life. Ideally, store and place things in ways that fit how and where you will use them, as this makes life easier. Keep the things you use the most closest to where you use them, and keep the things you use less often farthest from you.

One common question that comes up is: what do I do with duplicate, frequently used items that I use in various areas of my space? When duplicate items like scissors, tape, paper clips, note-pads, and pens are used in a child's room, the office, the kitchen, and the garage, you can distribute them to where they will be used the most, and find a permanent home for them within that area. However, be aware that keeping like items in too many different places will create disorientation. Part of what makes the Clutter Remedy strategy successful is that you always know where things are, since each type of object has a very specific, designated area. This helps you have a more calm and relaxing life.

For multiple duplicates that you want to keep, create a "mother-lode" area for extras of certain categories. For instance, when you own fifty lightbulbs, contain ten commonly used light-bulbs in an appropriate-sized clear bin in or near your laundry room, for easy access, and then put the rest in another container in the garage. Refill the laundry room bin as you use up your lightbulbs, and when purchasing more in bulk, put them in the garage bin.

When helping clients put things back into their space, I usually hear them say, "I've been looking for that for months." Searching for things you want to wear, use, or gift leads to a gnaw-ing feeling. It can lead to giving up the expedition and buying or ordering something you already own, again and again. With the Clutter Remedy strategy, there will be no more episodes where you can't find your keys, much less your windbreaker on a windy day. You want your belongings, stored near or far, easy to find.

The average time it takes to find things in cluttered, uncategorized spaces is fifteen to twenty minutes. The average time in an organized space is about two to three minutes.

Finally, take "after" pictures and compare them to your "before" pictures.

4

ROOM BY ROOM

Bedroom, Kitchen, Bathroom, Office

This chapter offers more specific advice for four of the most important, and sometimes the most challenging, spaces in the home to declutter and organize: the bedroom, kitchen, bathroom, and office.

A RESTFUL BEDROOM:
CALMING DOWN CLOTHES AND CLOSETS

As I mention in chapter 3, declutter and organize clothes in closets directly, after the rest of the bedroom is done, since all the hanging clothes will remain hanging until you go through and declutter them. Decluttering bedrooms is easy with the following strategies for calming those closets and dressers.

Whether you're dealing with hanging clothes in your closets

or clothing you have pulled out of dressers and cabinets and off the closet floor, first use broad categories to distinguish each type of clothing and accessory. Then fine-tune those categories by style, color, and season. Here are some sample categories:

Sample Broad Clothing/Accessory Categories

- Pants
- Shorts
- Skirts
- Dresses
- Suits
- Blouses
- Dress shirts
- Evening wear
- Sweaters
- Sweatshirts
- Jackets/Coats
- T-shirts
- Undergarments
- Pajamas
- Sports/activewear
- Cultural clothing
- Event clothing
- Jeans
- Leggings
- Purses
- Ties
- Belts
- Hats
- Scarves
- Shoes
- Jewelry

Categories by Season

- Winter
- Spring
- Summer
- Autumn

Categories by Color

- Red
- Blue
- Orange
- Yellow
- Green
- Black
- Brown
- Gray
- White
- Beige
- Pink
- Purple
- Magenta
- Maroon

As I said, start with broad categories, and then fine-tune by style, type, color, and season. Then determine piece by piece what you will keep, using the Clear and Concise Criteria. Some clothing is merely functional, or serves a specific purpose, and some clothing is like an old friend, faded, but it makes you happy to have it. However, avoid letting sentiment encourage you to keep once-favorite pieces that are now dated, worn-out, stained, ripped, or torn, or that don't fit your build or style anymore. Get objective and stylist advice about what to keep. See what makes you "pop." When it comes to unflattering clothing, my favorite phrase is "I'd rather not see you dead in that."

How to Store Clothes

As you put clothes away, keep evaluating whether each item meets the Clear and Concise Criteria. Ask yourself, "Do I wear this?" Even if you wear it only once a year, it's a "keep." Also ask, "Does it serve a purpose?" This would be like a uniform or specific work clothes that you wear regularly. Those are keeps. Ask, "Do I love it?" When you don't love something, ask yourself, "What is it doing in my real estate?" Finally, ask, "Is it sentimental?" Old T-shirts or a special-occasion dress can be sentimental, and these will end up with sentimental items outside of your closet space.

My preference and recommendation is to hang all clothes, including T-shirts and shorts, when there is ample space to hang clothes. I do not recommend placing clothing directly on a shelf, laid flat and stacked in a pile. Like all items, clothes are to be "contained" and stored so they don't "schmoosh." When clothes are piled, it is difficult to get to the clothing in the middle or at the bottom of the pile without messing up all the other folded clothing. Instead, fold items like shirts, jeans, and sweaters, and then roll them into a cylinder shape, which is what flight attendants do to maximize space in suitcases and to have wrinkle-free clothes.

Then, either in dresser drawers or in baskets on shelves, sort those clothes by type, style, color, and season. Depending on your container or space, place rolled items on end, rather than stacked, so you see the end of each roll. This way, you don't go digging into a rolled stack of clothes, disrupting all the other items.

For so-called undergarment drawers, use inserts to keep the various socks, underwear, boxer shorts, bras, and pantyhose separated, or store each type in its own basket or bin. Personally, I do not fold my undergarments or bras. I simply keep them in separate compartments of a drawer, but folding undergarments is a personal choice. For socks, I recommend pairing them and folding them together. I love rolling and placing ties and belts in shallow cloth bins, arranged by color and style, so you can clearly see them and keep them neat. I don't like hanging ties or belts, since they tend to flop around, fall on the floor, and get tangled. I recommend placing purses neatly in bins rather than directly on shelves, which protects them and keeps them categorized. If possible, I also recommend creating a separate shoe closet or cabinet that's near the home's entrance or garage. Of course, how you store shoes, clothing, and accessories will follow your own preferences and lifestyle, so long as everything is contained in fine-tuned categories and follows the Four Rules for an Organized Space (see page 76).

Indeed, in small bedrooms where space is limited, a smart strategy is to keep only the current season's clothing in your bedroom and store the rest in the back of your closet or in closed clear bins, which I discuss in chapter 5.

Once you have completely organized your bedroom and closet, I suggest decorating the closet area so that it reflects your personal style, whether that's "boutique," "boudoir," or "masculine." Reflect on your space and ask yourself, "Is this what I envisioned?" After all of the planning and carefully considered steps, you want your space to be perfectly paired to your taste.

THE COORDINATED KITCHEN

The kitchen is where most of the activity happens in a home. It is where you cook, eat, discuss the day's events, entertain, and open mail. Usually, when I have people over, no matter where I steer the guests, we always end up in the kitchen. Kitchen organization will make the daily chores of cooking and cleaning go smoother. Organizing the kitchen will make it easier to host gatherings and can even make you a better chef. Follow these steps to organize your kitchen quickly and efficiently.

The Food Pantry

I prefer a food pantry specifically used only for food products. But whether you keep food in a single pantry or a range of cabinets, categorize and organize food products the same way as with any other items. See below for dealing with refrigerators. Here is my "easy-peasy pantry category list":

Easy-Peasy Pantry Category List

- Protein (canned meats, fish, beans, peanut butter)
- Pasta
- Grains
- Vegetables (canned, dried, or bottled)
- Soup (canned or boxed)
- Breakfast (cereal, bars, oatmeal, pancake mix, muffin mix)
- Baking goods: flour, sugar, baking powder and soda
- Snacks (bars, crackers, chips, nuts)
- Fruit (canned, dried, or bottled)
- Sugar snacks/candy/cookies/desserts
- Condiments (ketchup, mustard, sauces, salad dressings)
- Spices
- Oils
- Vinegars
- Beverages

You could have other food categories, but the important thing is to categorize broadly and then fine-tune into subcategories. Remove all items from your pantry and cabinets, and categorize like with like: spices with spices, cereal with cereal, snacks with snacks, desserts with desserts. Separate all condiments with condiments, and soup with soup. Categorize by food product; don't categorize by can, jar, or any other shape. For example, tomato products — whether sun-dried tomatoes, canned tomatoes, tomato paste, or bottled tomato sauce — all belong together.

It's surprising what various items, besides human food, I find in pantries. I find vases, extra appliances, pots, pans, dishes, paper products, kids' schoolwork, medications, and even pet products. Ideally, reserve the food pantry for food, and get rid of old and expired products. Make sure herbs and spices are no older than one year. Oils are essentially spoiled at expiration, as are many other food products. Carefully read the dates on food.

When putting back what you will keep, place each food category into an open container; this makes it easy to pull them out of the pantry. Even if you have pull-out shelves, don't place food directly on a shelf, or categories will "schmoosh." I recommend shoe- and boot-size plastic bins that fit the size of the shelving. The bins also act as an inventory system; you will easily recognize when certain food items are diminishing.

Take food and drink products out of the boxes they are sold in and put them into open bins instead. When you take things out of bulky packaging, it is a major space saver. For instance, get rid of the boxes for cereal, health bars, instant oatmeal, snacks, drinks, and generally anything that comes in an oversized box. For cereal, the clear bag takes less space, and you can clearly see which cereal is which; use clips to keep the cereal fresh, and line up all the cereal bags in a bin, the correct size for the amount of cereal you have. Individually wrapped items, like health bars, are removed from their box. Even loose foods like cookies and candy can be transferred to zipped plastic bags, rather than staying in bulky boxes. Put all categorized and contained food in bins. Do the same with tea bags: Transfer types of tea into zipped plastic bags and place the bags in a bin; for unmarked tea, cut the tea name from the box and place it in the zipped bag. However, for boxed food items with instructions, such as pancake or cake mix, keep them in their boxes, unless you're familiar with the preparation of the products. Then again, when space is tight, you can cut off the instructions and put the food pouch and instructions together in a large zipped plastic bag. These strategies save you time and space.

Once everything is categorized into bins, place them in the pantry by how often you use them. Items most frequently used stay on shelves that are easiest to reach, while less-used items are placed toward the back of the pantry or on less-accessible shelving. Frequently used spices can be kept in a nearby drawer or cabinet, while those used less often can be stored farther away. Extra or bulk food products, or what isn't used on a regular basis, are placed in categorized bins in a farther storage area, like a garage. Do not overfill bins since you can stack them to save space. For instance, you could stack an open light bin of snacks on top of an open bin of health bars.

I prefer bins where you can see the food products clearly. Bins made out of plastic material are inexpensive and easy to clean versus, for instance, wire baskets. Whatever containment you choose, though, is your preference.

Cookware and Dishware

I recommend emptying and categorizing all drawers first, and then doing the cabinets next. Be careful reaching into high areas, and always have someone spot you on a stool or ladder.

In addition, at every stage of kitchen organization, once

everything is removed from shelves, cabinets, and drawers, including the refrigerator, thoroughly clean before putting bins back and refilling shelves. Wipe down all surfaces and drawers, and consider lining shelves and drawers with a paper you find attractive. To me, nice thick wallpaper is always a treat as shelf paper.

Once all cabinets and drawers are empty, divide everything into broad categories, choose what you will keep, and figure out where everything will go based on use. As with clothing, I recommend getting rid of old, chipped, mismatched dishware and burnt, worn cookware. Some items will have sentimental value, but ensure each item still functions properly and is used. I do not recommend keeping any pots or pans with toxic materials, which can be scraped off into food, or any aluminum products. I recommend nontoxic products such as stainless steel, glass, ceramic, or "green" products.

Place the pots and pans you use the most in the front of the cabinet, and put occasionally used pots and pans in the back. Separate lids from pan bottoms, and store them on separate shelves or side by side near one another. Keep items used often close to where you will use them. For instance, place a cutting board near the trash can and knives near the cutting board. Put pot holders in a drawer near the oven and stove, and coffee cups close to the coffee machine.

When you have deep cabinets that go far back, invest in pull-out shelves or a revolving corner shelf. I once became caught in a deep, narrow, lower corner cabinet reaching for a Bundt pan. The more I panicked, the more I puffed up and became stuck. After that, I did not count that part of the cabinet as usable space until it was modified.

Store the bottoms of plastic and glass food storage containers inside one another, sorted by shape and size. Keep the tops of storage containers, separated by shape and size, in zipped plastic bags for easy access. Separating bottoms from tops saves space and time. Grab the bottom first and then find the coordinating top. Cookbooks that you use regularly can be stored in a higher cabinet above the stove or decoratively on the countertop, two to three at the most.

As for dishware, I recommend keeping matching sets (for example, of four or eight or more). I believe having matching sets of silverware, glassware, and dishes induces a feeling of calm, but some people prefer for each glass and plate to be unique, and that's fine when it creates happy feelings. Store glasses, bowls, dishes, and silverware in the cabinets nearest to the dishwasher, so they are easy to unload and put away.

When you have too much of one particular item for your immediate space, regardless of whether it is food, bulky appliances, entertainment pieces, or things you only use occasionally, store them in larger clear bins with a secure lid in the garage or storage area or in a cabinet near the kitchen.

Remove or Organize Nonkitchen Items

Do not keep or store anything that does not belong in the kitchen area, such as bills, important papers, toys, office supplies, tools, and school or work stuff. These items are better placed with like items elsewhere, and where they are generally used, whether that's in an office desk or cabinet, playroom, garage, utility cabinet, or storage area. I do not recommend keeping bills or important papers in kitchen drawers unless your office desk is in the kitchen area. Place bills and important paperwork where you can sit and process them easily and effectively.

Of course, you can keep a "junk" drawer of go-to, nonkitchen items: keys, sunglasses, scissors, tape measure, notepads, and pens. But organize that drawer like every other storage space in the house. Turn that "junk" drawer into a "neat" drawer. Use drawer inserts that separate items by fine-tuned categories for ultimate organization. Any items that are meant to be permanently stored in the kitchen are to be categorized and contained. Remember, this approach is not about being "neat," although that's a plus. It's about getting and staying organized, so you will find what you want when you want to use it by creating a place for every item and always putting items back where they belong.

People have a tendency to dump things on countertops, especially in the kitchen, but also in the laundry room and on dining tables and couches. Humans are natural-born pilers. So I recommend making places for temporary piles that are discreet and hidden from view. This can be inside a "neat" empty drawer; for newspapers, magazines, mail, and flyers, create a "stash" container or basket with a lid. Then be sure to look through, process, and organize stashed items regularly. When the laundry room is where things are dumped, have a lidded basket that you go through regularly. Wherever you are piling, get a basket or bin, so you are not breaking the second rule of my Four Rules for an Organized Space (see page 76).

Free kitchen countertops of any items unless they are aesthetically pleasing or used daily, such as a coffeemaker, juicer, toaster, and a few décor items. Be sure to have a place to put daily, nonaesthetic items away when you have company over. A clear countertop looks better and gives you more space for cooking and entertaining. Contain vitamins, aspirin, cold medicine, and other medications separately; although they can be used daily, they are better stored out of sight. When you see medications regularly, it tells your subconscious mind to "get sick." On the other hand, although vitamins and regular prescriptions are something you want to take, keep them discreetly tucked away, out of sight.

Refreshing the Refrigerator

Clear and organize the refrigerator the same way as every other "storing area": Empty it completely, categorize items, choose what you will keep, and then contain all like items together. Containing food categories makes it easier to keep refrigerator shelves clean and sanitized at all times. Like in a food pantry, storing categories of food in clear, easy to pull out bins acts as an inventory control system, and it's easy to retrieve food to bring to your countertop. No more digging through the fridge for ketchup or capers.

Refrigerators do not keep food from spoiling indefinitely. Prior to going to the market, check your inventory and check for any spoiled food. If you have the slightest doubt about food, don't risk it. Throw it out and buy new. Before placing bins back into the refrigerator, clean and sanitize the entire inside.

LAVISHING YOUR LAVATORY

You declutter and organize a bathroom using the same strategy, yet bathrooms generally have very little storage space, and they usually contain a wide range of small items. In a bathroom, categorizing every little thing and strategizing containment can take hours to get correct. In any case, it's worth it since it will cut the time to get ready in the morning in half. Start by clearing out all drawers, cabinets, and medicine cabinets; divide everything into broad categories; clean the empty space thoroughly; line shelves and place drawer inserts into drawers; figure out what to keep; and fine-tune it. Here is a sample list of broad bathroom categories:

Sample Broad Category List for Bathrooms

- Dental/oral
- Ear
- Eye
- Facial skin care
- Lotions (hand, body)
- Bathtub accessories
- Deodorant
- Hair products
- Cologne (for men)
- Perfume (for women)
- Facial tissue
- Toilet paper
- Cotton balls
- Shower caps

- Shaving
- Makeup
- Lip balm
- Nail items
- Medicinal items
- Cleaning products
- Hand soap
- Body wash
- Powder
- Tweezers

- Electronics (dryers, irons, shavers)
- Travel kits
- Wet wipes
- Sanitizers
- Towels (bath, hand, and washcloths)
- Robes
- Floor mats
- Shower mats

After you have broadly categorized your bathroom contents, start fine-tuning. For example, within the category of makeup, fine-tune by color lipstick with lipstick, blush with blush, foundation with foundation, and eye shadow with eye shadow. With hair products, fine-tune all with like, for instance, shampoo with shampoo, hair color with hair color, sprays with sprays, pomades with pomades, and brushes with brushes. The process is eye-opening. People tend to have a lot of specific products, more than they realized, while discovering half finished but no longer used products they forgot about long ago.

When it comes to deciding what products stay or go, be discriminating, based on whether you have ever or will ever use them. Some bathroom products are expired or simply old, dried out, or tired. Some can last forever, but ask yourself, "Will I ever use this?" For bathroom products, consider whether they still match your current style. People can be reluctant to throw out makeup and care products because they are expensive, but if you don't and won't use something, ask yourself, "what's it doing in my real estate?" Keep the things that you use, that serve a purpose, and that you love.

Many health, beauty, and skin-care products contain harmful and toxic chemicals that are dangerous to your health and better to be disposed of responsibly. Review the ingredients on all labels. Expensive lotions will promise to make you appear younger, yet a close look at the labels can reveal ingredients known to cause dry skin, wrinkles, dermatitis, dandruff, and irritations; some can affect your hormones and metabolism. I always recommend using natural products. I prefer natural hair dyes made from plant extracts and natural creams made from coconut, cocoa butter, jojoba, and olive oil, which effectively heal dry skin. Look for shampoos, conditioners, teeth products, and deodorants without harsh ingredients. Use your best judgment and research harmful ingredients in beauty products.

Symbolizing collections is very useful when decluttering bathrooms. Marina discovered she had eleven hairbrushes, five curling irons, three hair dryers, and every kind of hair product imaginable. For Marina, all her hair brushes and hair products symbolized becoming "more beautiful." Yet when she considered whether they actually did make her more beautiful, the answer was "no." Most of her tools and products dried and damaged her hair. So Marina disposed of everything harmful and old and re-placed them with natural hair products and a single brush, hair dryer, and curling iron specifically designed for her hair type. Soon her hair was restored to a healthy, shiny, beautiful state. Marina realized her inner and outer beauty had nothing do with her beauty products.

When it comes to containment and storing bathroom sup-plies, get creative in terms of configuring the available space. In addition to keeping categories contained and assigning every-thing a designated home, you want to keep the things you use the most within easy reach. For instance, storing toilet paper and feminine products near the toilet is a cherished convenience, as is storing your toothbrush and razor near the sink and the mirror. When space is limited, it sometimes helps to keep a smaller bot-tle or amount nearby for everyday use, and then placing bulk or refill containers, and seldom-used products, in a nearby cabinet or closet.

Ideally you want clear, manageable space that's easy to access.

DEVELOPING A DIVINE OFFICE SPACE

"I can't find my..." "Somebody moved my..." "Who took my...?" Does this sound familiar? Whether you are organizing a home office or business office, the key to success is feeling coordinated, comfortable, and focused. Mixing business into your home space can be done with splendor while conducting business with dignity and control. Offices, like bathrooms, tend to be complicated spaces that take longer to organize. Again, this is well worth your time. Plus, people often struggle with organizing their important papers, which I treat as a separate, related project.

Step One: Categorize and Organize the Office

As with any other room, start by emptying all the contents of the entire work space and categorizing items into clear bins. Form the broad categories, choose what to keep using the Clear and Concise Criteria, and then fine-tune everything into subcategories. The only exception is paper — initially, gather together all mail, bills, publications, photos, notes, and papers of any kind, set them aside, and fine-tune and organize them after everything else in the space is done and put away. It's more efficient to review and organize papers separately in a clear and organized space (see pages 96–100).

After fine-tuning, identify types of containment, and figure out storing areas based on use. For instance, if you use paper clips regularly, contain them all in the same zipped plastic bag, bowl, or small container, and place them in your immediate space. If paper clips of a certain size or type are rarely used, contain them separately and store them outside your immediate space. Within your immediate space, such as a desk drawer, keep only high-use materials — those used daily, weekly, or monthly — each one categorized and separated by drawer organizers, zipped plastic bags, or containers. Store occasionally or rarely used items, such as extra office supplies or reference books, out of your immediate space, so they don't get in the way of high-use items. This makes the space airier and more usable.

Discard responsibly any outdated office supplies — like dried-up bottles of glue. When you have ten staplers or sixteen scissors, ask yourself, "What is a reasonable number?" If an item is used, purposeful, sentimental, or loved, it's a keeper. I recommend keeping decorative items, pictures, and photos that are uplifting, since these liven up the space with positive energy. However, in general, nonoffice items do not belong in a work space, so find a more suitable home for them.

As you arrange items in the office and on the desk, envision what you do and how you work on a regular basis. When you use a stapler and calculator daily, place them on the desktop. When you use things weekly, move them to a drawer. For rarely used items, place them in a cabinet across the room. Use this same approach for files, paper, magazines, and books: Keep those things you access frequently within your reach next to or within your desk. Little-used files and books are to be stored separately on a nearby shelf or cabinet. Arrange the furniture to ensure good energy and flow. Ideally, position your desk so you are facing the door, like the "office of the president," which is the power position.

Step Two: Organize Important Papers

I get the most complaints about paper, which is a source of constant woe, but to me, paper is the easiest thing to categorize, organize, and eliminate. Paper is light, for one, and important papers do not take up much space. Creating an individualized filing system will take patience, yet once done, it's easy to maintain and adjust. Once paper is organized, it only becomes the enemy when it is neglected. Even tax season is less stressful, since you will be regularly categorizing bills and receipts as you go, year-round. If you're stuck in paper misery, don't fear. However, this is why I recommend tackling paper separately, since organizing paper often sidetracks people from organizing the rest of their space.

The biggest question is deciding which papers to keep and which to throw away or shred. Some papers are easily discarded, like junk mail; some papers are meant to be kept only temporarily; and some papers are to be kept for life.

First, categorize each and every piece of paper, which makes going through them much easier. It can sometimes be challenging to process paper without getting emotionally charged. As you categorize, avoid focusing on the content of the paperwork; don't read anything during this part of the strategy. This is the biggest factor for categorizing papers quickly and efficiently. Also make sure you have a large table or floor area and many plastic bins for sorting. Sort all papers categorically: receipts with receipts, bills with bills, bank statements with bank statements, notes with notes, business cards with business cards, and all like papers with like papers. Then fine-tune those categories, first by date and then by use and purpose. You will come across sentimental papers, like photos, and those become a category that you will ultimately want to fine-tune. Determine when things are functional, sentimental, or for display, such as old calendars, appointment books, memorabilia, cards, doodles, and letters from loved ones. Fine-tuning stored memorabilia can be done as a "to do" project. However, don't do this task until your overall project is complete.

Once the papers are sufficiently categorized, choose what to keep. For papers that are meant to be kept temporarily (such as documents related to annual taxes), shred whatever is too old, while keeping pertinent papers that you will refer back to. Some papers only pertain to certain purchases or circumstances; when you no longer own a particular car or appliance or no longer have the same health insurance, toss the papers associated with it.

Here are two lists to consider. The first lists documents that are kept temporarily; the second lists documents you will keep for life.

Papers to Keep Temporarily

- Receipts and papers for taxes (keep tax records for at least eight years)
- Pay stubs (keep at least a year; more if getting a bank loan)
- Receipts for recent purchases
- Current bill or invoice statement(s), no more than past three months
- Records for patients or clients that are required by law
- Current passwords
- Current vehicle information, including title, loan documents, and auto registration cards
- Current banking and credit card statements (keep at least a year; more if getting a bank loan)
- Legal documents you are currently working on
- Medical records and bills (keep at least a year for tax purposes; longer for disputes)
- Current newsletters or calendar of events
- Current coupons
- Business cards
- Home improvement and home sale documents (keep at least six years after a home sale)
- Notes
- Warranties for current products (keep for as long as you own the item)
- Annual insurance policy
- Retirement plan (401k), 529, IRA, etc.

Papers to Keep for Life

- Birth and death certificates
- Social security cards
- Password and identification (ID) cards
- Pension plan documents
- Health records for chronic challenges
- Passports
- Marriage license
- Business and/or professional licenses
- Any life insurance policy or policies
- Wills, living wills, and documents pertaining to divorce, child support/custody, adoption, and powers of attorney
- House deeds and mortgage documents
- Very special and sentimental letters/cards, photos, children's artwork
- Scholarly achievements (degrees/diplomas)

Let's face it, processing papers can take up precious time and be tedious, unless you categorize them first. While some people love their hard copies, I recommend developing a paperless system as much as you can. By regularly scanning documents and receipts with a printer, or taking pictures with a smartphone, you can keep them safe and avoid stressful searches for misplaced paper. That said, you can't go paperless with all documents. This includes everything in the "papers to keep for life" list above, along with any documents pertaining to your business for state and federal purposes. Ideally, keep your most important papers in a metal box, a metal filing cabinet, or a safe-deposit box. When storing things digitally, remember to regularly back up scans and pictures of important papers. All other papers are to be organized into a filing system with labeled folders. Organize this filing system in whatever way suits you, but as a general rule, put papers and folders you refer to frequently toward the front of each drawer, while papers you use less frequently can be arranged in the back. Devise a system that matches how you prepare your tax information every year. Filing receipts for expenses, tracking payments, and organizing any other tax documents throughout the year will make it much easier for you, or your tax professional, to complete this chore when the time comes.

As new mail and papers arrive, do not put them directly on surfaces, on furniture, or on the floor. Place decorative baskets, bins, or containers where you tend to plop them, creating temporary holding places until you sort, categorize, file, or dispose of them. Sort mail as it arrives, since most of it can go directly into the recycling bin, or make a regular habit of going through "the mail basket," before it becomes overwhelming. Remember, for every type of document you keep, create some type of containment. To store business cards, keep them in a box or zipped bag, or photograph them to keep them permanently stored digitally. Most of the papers people tend to file they never look at again. I regard keeping paper you never refer to as a form of overcollecting.

Also, be proactive about eliminating paper. All banking, credit card, and insurance companies store your account information, which can be accessed online. Many schools, religious organizations, investment companies, professional organizations, and social clubs are going paperless and sending electronic newsletters, or they give you the option. Many magazines and newspapers can be read online. Avoiding paper means mounting paper clutter, which is notorious for creeping into your space daily.

Christine had not processed her papers for over fifteen years. When I entered her large office space and guest room — where she had stashed all the piled-up receipts, taxes, music she wrote, statements, and hundreds of little notes with random phone numbers, scribbles, and thoughts — I was astonished at the volume of paper she had. When categorizing her papers, we saw that Christine had even written a note in pencil on the sheer paper of a dry cleaner's wire hanger. We laughed hysterically that she had the expert note-taking ability to master the penciled note without poking a hole through the sheer paper. After categorizing all like papers with like papers using the Clear and Concise Criteria, Christine ended up keeping only a small stack of papers that were mostly sentimental and papers she used for work.

When you find the task of processing paper abhorrent and aggravating, get some help to gather it up and make sense of it with care and confidence.

5

PERPETUAL
ORGANIZATION
YEAR-ROUND

Once you complete the Clutter Remedy strategy in your space, the goal becomes staying organized and maintaining that organizational system. Perpetual organization doesn't just happen, and it's not a one-time process. It takes ongoing commitment and flexibility, attention and willingness, throughout the year. Each season brings its own changes: in the weather and in the ebb and flow of work, school, and holidays. In addition, paying attention to how you shop will help you keep your space clutter-free. When you decide to move, or when you're going through a major life transition — a job change, children leaving for college, retirement, or grief and loss — these events present unique challenges, and you will want to make regular adjustments. Finally, families with children, especially young children, will be making perpetual adjustments as children reach certain milestones. This chapter looks at all these situations and offers suggestions for how to stay organized with ease and grace despite the inevitable, regular disruptions to your year-round routines.

STAYING ORGANIZED
THROUGH THE SEASONS

The seasons often involve what I call "musical stuff." That is, they indicate what specific clothes you will wear and stuff you will use, so your things continually dance around to the music of the weather as they rotate in and out of use. You don't want pool toys around in the dead of winter or ski boots in your face in the middle of August. You don't want closets and bedroom furniture stuffed with every piece of clothing you own. You want your wardrobe to reflect the current season. This way your clothes and accessories are easy to access. When your belongings are fine-tuned and contained, whether it is clothing or kitchen items, gardening tools, sports equipment, or kid stuff, it makes it easy to move things near or far depending on what you are using at any given time, so that you keep nearby only what you want for that season, and you move nonseasonal items to less-accessible storing areas.

The changing seasons affect us as well. You start to notice seasonal transitions two to three weeks before the end of the current season, and this transition often lasts for another few weeks into the new season. These transitions trigger what I call a "seasonal pull," or a temporary feeling of being pulled in a different direction. Within these periods in-between seasons, the weather changes, and your activity level and focus shift. You can experience insomnia or oversleeping and changes in your appetite. Being aware of and adapting to these changes will keep you focused on remaining organized in all aspects of your life.

Autumn

Autumn is full of energy, movement, and vitality. It is a season of new beginnings. After summer vacations, adults head back to work, and kids return to school. For families, the hustle and bustle of back-to-school shopping starts fall off with a bang. With kids, establish organized routines before school starts, and anticipate that last year's school and homework routines will change as kids get older.

Autumn calls for a shift in clothing. Summer clothes, like bathing suits, sandals, and shorts, are worn less; sweaters, long sleeves, and pants come back into play. Reposition your seasonal clothes. This will mean putting summer clothes at the back of closets or moving them in closed clear bins to more distant storing areas, like the garage, basement, attic, or a guest-room closet.

In addition, with every seasonal transition, use this opportunity to go through last year's clothing and weed out whatever you haven't worn, don't plan to wear, and will never wear. Using the Clear and Concise Criteria, evaluate every item as you pull it out. Go through shoes, boots, coats, leggings, socks, sweaters, and jeans. Do any have holes? Does everything still fit? Has your style changed? What items do you still love? If you choose to keep a piece of clothing for sentimental reasons but don't plan to wear it, then don't place it in your immediate space.

Autumn includes two major holidays that are synonymous with food, decorating, and socializing: Halloween and Thanksgiving. Go all out with Halloween décor if you want, but only to the extent that you enjoy it. Don't sacrifice your peace of mind and the peace of your space by overcluttering it with holiday decorations. Similarly, be careful not to overindulge in candy and sweets, which affect mood and energy. Keeping large bowls of candy out during Halloween can be dangerous, since eating too much sugar causes lethargy, which will make it harder to keep up your space. Anything that gets in the way of your motivation to stay organized and support your life goals is to be avoided, which means maintaining a healthy diet.

What about Thanksgiving? Indeed, this celebrated holiday is defined by overindulgence. For many, Thanksgiving dinner means turkey, cranberries, sweet potatoes, marshmallows, stuffing, gravy, green bean casserole, bread, and pie — a meal most would never eat in any other circumstance. Organizing your diet during this time will involve self-discipline and perhaps saving some food items for the next day. That's what leftovers are all about.

Winter

December is dominated by the holiday season, which often involves lots of parties, visitors, travel, and special meals. Maintaining an organized home is a particular challenge this month, given all the pressure to decorate, buy presents, host gatherings, and cook. This is when having a fine-tuned storing system will help a great deal, since it makes it much easier to find all those special-occasion holiday items.

Family tradition calls for extravagant holiday displays, and if that's what you enjoy and prefer, by all means pull out everything and go to town. However, when you feel overwhelmed, busy, or disorganized, I recommend keeping things simple. Unpack and put up only half of the holiday decorations you normally put up. String a portion of your lights and get a smaller tree. Put out only some of your special-occasion bowls, vases, and platters, along with only a few scented candles. I guarantee you will feel more rested, at ease, and enjoy the festivities.

People often resist this advice. With a heavy-hearted whine, they say they "do it for the kids." However, if decorating induces a merry meltdown, reconsider this reasoning. Do kids enjoy watching their parents stress out about what tree to buy and where to put it, running around hunting for family heirloom ornaments while enforcing good cheer? No, they would rather have relaxed and communicative parents who are genuinely content.

Every time holiday decorations come out, go through them and declutter whatever does not make you feel jolly. Similarly, when each season's décor comes out, evaluate decorations and donate or responsibly dispose of anything that has become tired, worn, frayed, or broken.

After the holiday season, many people struggle with the "New Year blues" due to excess sugar consumption, overdoing it, lack of sleep, and a lower-than-usual bank account. When this happens to you, putting your space back in order will help lift your energy level, and you will feel the contentment of getting back to "normal." Do it at a pace that is comfortable without pushing yourself. As I say, "When you push, you fall." And remember, "perpetual organization" doesn't mean that clutter never appears again. It simply means that your space is organized and restored regularly in ways that allow it to be maintained easily.

Another thing about the new year is that it brings the process of self-evaluation. You will naturally look back on the previous year and consider successes and failures, and then you will look ahead, set goals, and seek to improve yourself with "New Year's resolutions" and realizations. I recommend using the start of the year to return to the exercises in chapter 1. Get out a pen and reflect on your values and life goals; consider how you will organize your home and your life better to achieve what you want. Perpetual organization means being flexible and adapting your organizational strategies to support your desires. What is still working for you, and what isn't anymore? What new things do you want to accomplish, and what changes will you make to get there? Focus on positive goals. Think about joining a charity, getting healthier, learning a language, engaging in more socializing, traveling to visit family, starting a business, or writing a book. Every year, creating an ideal lifestyle list enhances your life. This is a magical wish list. Don't be afraid to dream big. Think large to create your own ideal lifestyle every year. You change every single moment, every single day, so keep thinking and writing about what you want out of life. Be the conductor of your life.

Spring

Spring is a beautiful time of year, and warmer weather is often the inspiration for spring cleaning. I recommend taking this seasonal opportunity to do a thorough dusting and vacuuming job. Then, as you air out the house, declutter as well, identifying, donating, and gifting any viable items that don't meet the Clear and Concise Criteria, while responsibly disposing of items that are obsolete, old, and worn-out.

Vacuum and clear dust from under and around beds, baseboards, closet shelves, draperies, and blinds. Vacuum underneath couches and all your furniture, moving furniture as necessary to get all the dust up and out of your space. Clean rugs, carpets, and upholstery, and clean the windows. Dust your fans, lamps, and lightbulbs; clean your oven and stove. Go the extra step and get rid of dust bunnies in corners of ceilings and from the tops of large pieces of furniture. The amount of dust we breathe is mind-boggling. I find people with intense allergies are not dusting and vacuuming regularly. Clean the washing machine, coffeemaker, and dishwasher with some white vinegar, and make sure your dryer and HVAC vents are clear of dust and debris. Polish your wood furniture and clean all your glass. Clean up house plants, cut back overgrown outdoor plants, and hose down patio areas.

Know that having an organized life is not all about categorizing and arranging things. It's also about keeping a clean and sanitized home indoors and out. Your home reflects you. How you are doing on an emotional level will manifest in your living space. If a home is *never* cleaned and becomes filthy, this is considered to be living in squalor. To me, that means the people living in squalid homes are most likely experiencing inner squalor, or what's called "a dark night of the soul." In order to improve their living conditions, people living in perpetually dirty, chaotic environments will want to clear out their emotional clutter. Whatever your situation, spring is a great time to put the sparkle and effervescence back into your life.

Summer

Summer is the season for enjoyment and soaking in the sun. It is a time to rest and relax, and it's a great time to get organized. You can do something fun and go on vacation, but staying home and getting organized could be very beneficial. Whether you're traveling or reorganizing your closets, either way, have fun! It is summer, for heaven's sake!

Summer vacations and parties can disrupt your regular organizational routines, and clutter can start to return. If this happens, go with the flow and gently *will* yourself to put things back in order. You know, with the Clutter Remedy strategy there is always a quick way and plenty of opportunities to restore good habits. Instead of taking a big, expensive trip, staying home and staying organized could be more restorative and often more satisfying and restful than traipsing across country. There is also something smart and wonderful about doing fun day trips in your own neck of the woods and sleeping in your own bed. Explore your area: Find new places to eat, and seek farmer's markets and local farms for fresh, organic, seasonal fruits and vegetables. This is delicious for the body and good for the soul. Then swim, bike, walk, and get your body moving. Take advantage of every opportunity to pursue healthy, fun activities and even find new ways to shop.

SMART SHOPPING: AVOID OVERACCUMULATION AND SHOP GREEN

Shopping can often become a frenzied, harried experience, and it can be a trap for buying things that don't support your lifestyle or fit in your space. When shopping, always use the Clear and Concise Criteria to prevent overaccumulation. Ask yourself while shopping: Will I use this? What purpose will it serve? Is this a sentimental purchase? Do I love it?

When you use these criteria, you will find yourself walking out of a store empty-handed, having avoided buying items that will quickly become clutter. Of course, there's nothing wrong with buying new stuff, especially when replacing old stuff that's outdated, but becoming a self-aware shopper helps avoid buyer's remorse. Marketing and advertising influence the "I want it now" mentality, which can foolishly lead to buying things you never wanted in the first place.

I am a "green shopper," and what I recommend for everyone is to "shop green." This means, rather than buying new, always look for and favor products that are recycled or slightly used. I only buy something new if there are no alternatives. First I go to thrift and consignment stores, garage sales, and flea markets. Some will laugh and call me cheap, but I love being frugal, and that's another benefit of green shopping: not overspending. This can be another way to support your values and life goals, by ensuring that less money is going out than is coming in, especially when large purchases of new stuff are a significant expense.

I have astonished my friends with the upscale, one-of-a-kind items I've found for pennies on the dollar. Brand-new, never-used vintage and designer clothes, shoes, and accessories can be found at thrift and consignment shops, estate sales, and through online resale websites. I've found designer hats, scarves, coats, skirts, pants, suits, and gloves all by green shopping. Best of all, I always feel delighted when I find luxurious, beautiful keepsakes without having to pay big bucks. The same is true for furniture pieces. I once bought a pair of antique marble nightstands for $120, and later I found them retailing online for $1,200 each. My dining table and chairs retail for $10,000 new, but I paid $700 for a lightly used set.

Some people cringe at the idea of thrift stores and green shopping. It's not for everyone, and you will find your own balance between what makes you comfortable and what is affordable, appropriate, and prudent. Be creative in the way you shop, so that you avoid clutter and overbuying while remaining economical and environmentally sound. Shop locally, shop green, and shop smart. Buy from local artisans, and support charities.

MANAGING A MOVE

There is a lot to do when planning and organizing for a move. The two aspects I focus on here are packing and assessing the new space.

Depending on the situation, hiring a Clutter Remedy expert organizer who specializes in move management could be a smart idea, especially when you want to downsize your belongings at the same time. Figuring out what you want to take is easier with an objective eye around, and a professional who has managed thousands of moves can identify furniture that's not worth moving and help you sell or donate those items. Organizers will also help you strategize new furniture and storage solutions before you move and when you arrive in the new place. Use the process of planning and preparation to minimize the inevitable stress of a move, whether you're moving across the country or down the street.

Declutter and Organize as You Pack

Before packing and moving, I recommend following the Clutter Remedy strategy in this book. Empty every room, categorize all of your belongings, and decide what to take versus what you will donate, sell, or dispose of. Then combine organizing, containment, and packing into one activity: Fine-tune your categories, contain each type of item, and pack everything into clear bins. Packing into clear bins is not only a greener option, since you can reuse them for storing items later, but you avoid the tedious task of procuring and putting together boxes, taping and marking them, and breaking them down and disposing of them on the other end. It makes unpacking a breeze since you can clearly see the contents of each bin and identify which area of the house they belong in. Since all your belongings are already categorized, fine-tuned, and contained, putting everything away in your new place is easy rather than stressful. When you are fortunate to have what I call "moving day" friends, ask for their help during this process.

Once you know your move date, start packing immediately, and schedule times for packing that fit your work and life schedule. Pack in stages or whenever you have a free hour or two. Don't leave packing for the last minute, since that's cumbersome and overwhelming.

Start by organizing and packing the items you will not be using prior to moving. This includes everything that's currently in storing areas of your current space, like the garage, attic, basement, sheds, guest closets, and under the stairwell. Start packing extra bedding and linens, rarely used kitchenware, seasonal decorations, and any memorabilia. Do as much as you can with your existing schedule to assess, declutter, and organize every box and bin you will be moving with.

When your move includes off-site storage filled with things that have not been used in years, that aren't serving a purpose, and that are not sentimental or loved any longer, use the Clutter Remedy strategy to figure out why you are holding on to items you never see or engage with. Many people I work with share that their storage unit is their "dirty little secret." When I ask them to symbolize the unit, their answers are generally that the storage represents "hidden" and "shameful" aspects of their life. Storage units are meant to be temporary, unless you have no on-site storage, yet I know people who have kept storage units and not opened them up for thirty years. Liza, who has had a storage unit for over twenty years, said, "For all I know, everything in there is molded and has disintegrated." Could this be symbolic of a locked-up and lost part of herself? Storage units can be expensive, so use the Clear and Concise Criteria to make good decisions about what to pack and what to release.

Before packing, collect bubble wrap, old newspapers, and packing paper from family, friends, and neighbors. In addition, use your linens, pillows, tablecloths, and towels to pack and cushion breakables.

Finally, don't pack any items you use daily, weekly, or monthly until closer to the move day, so that you will not feel inconvenienced in any way.

Assess the New Space and Your Furniture

In the same way that you visualize and assess your current space in the Clutter Remedy strategy (see pages 53–54), do the same in your new home. Use or create a floor plan of the entire new space, including window and door placement, and assess all the storing areas and closets. Then assess and measure all your current furniture to see how it will fit into your new space, style- and size-wise. Use the Clear and Concise Criteria, and donate or sell any furniture that is not useful or purposeful in the new space. When there are sentimental and loved pieces you won't part with, take them, and feel confident you can repurpose or use them somewhere, even if they will not fit the new architecture and décor. Don't leave behind things you cherish. You will find a place for them, and if they absolutely will not work out, gift them to friends or family, so they will remain around for you to visit and admire.

Assessing the new home, your furniture, and how everything will be placed and organized will save you time, effort, and money on move-in day. What fits in your current home can be awkward in the new one. As importantly, understanding any differences in storage areas between your current home and the new one will help you make good decisions about what storage pieces to keep. If there's less storage space, you can buy new furniture to hold all your belongings, or you can find secondhand solutions, such as bookshelves or armoires. Ask yourself, "What's the best way to store my stuff?" Then consider what furniture, closets, cabinets, armoires, dressers, drawers, storage ottomans, chests, and decorative receptacles you will find and utilize to store all the stuff you love.

A perfect example of an ill-fated move was when Nate moved from a 1950s condominium to a modern town house. Prior to the move, Nate gave away and sold a lot of his furniture, thinking he didn't want it any longer and that it didn't fit the look of the new town house. He thought newer space meant better space; he was enamored by the new place's fancy appliances, granite countertops, and shiny cabinets. However, Nate never measured the space or considered where all his belongings would go. His 1950s condo housed deep, built-in cabinets on every wall and had plentiful closets, while the town house had one tiny entryway closet, no built-ins, two small master-bedroom closets, and one small closet in the guest room. A very small linen cabinet was barely deep enough to hold folded towels and sheets. The small kitchen cabinets were insufficient to hold all of Nate's cookware, dishes, and entertaining pieces. Nate was an avid cook who loved to entertain, so kitchen storage was important for him.

Nate hadn't budgeted for buying new furniture, and as I and my team helped him unpack, he became highly agitated and upset. There was nowhere to put anything, and no magic wand that would miraculously create storage space that didn't exist. Happily, I helped Nate do some green shopping online and at consignment stores, and we soon found some affordable armoires, cabinets, and garage shelving that matched the town house's floor plan and architecture and that provided adequate, accessible storage for all of his things. When the new furniture arrived, Nate realized his old stuff would not have worked anyway, even if he'd kept it, yet he would have saved himself trouble and angst by planning ahead and truly understanding the scope of his new space.

Julia also did not plan her move well. She relocated from Chicago to Los Angeles for an exciting job opportunity, and she decided to take every single thing she owned with her. Prior to moving, Julia looked for a new home in Los Angeles, and she became enthralled with and bought a glamorous Mediterranean-style home. Yet she never assessed the architecture or floor plan. Julia's traditional, antique furniture matched her colonial-style home in Chicago, but in her LA house, the same furniture looked old, scuffed up, and unattractive; the furniture didn't fit well and was completely out of place in her new home, nor was it truly special or valuable. It was like putting a square peg into a round hole. Julia sat and cried about all the money she had spent moving everything across the country and how awful it looked in the new home. Though she felt foolish and guilty, she realized the easy remedy was to sell and donate what she had and start fresh.

Ultimately, having the perfect furniture is not a life-or-death situation. When you move, identifying usable space for everything you want to keep is important for creating a clutter-free environment. Take your time to find good storage solutions that work for your stuff and that create good aesthetics for the space. Feeling stressed about making the new place look great immediately will only lead to poor decision-making. I tell clients it can take up to three years to make a new home or office great. Plan ahead and do what you can, without pushing yourself. I say, "When you push, you fall." To make your new place the best it can be, take it slowly, make well-thought-out choices, know your "today taste" (which you will learn about in chapter 6), and remember that it does not happen overnight.

DOWNSIZING: DECLUTTERING DURING LIFE TRANSITIONS

Any life transition can spur a desire to downsize and to peruse and assess accumulated clutter and memorabilia: Moving, decreased income, empty nest, marriage, birth of a child, divorce, loss of function, and retiring are common transitions. Typically, during life transitions, we shift from one stage of life to another, and our priorities and even our sense of self will change. We can have the urge to purge and start fresh, along with a reluctance to eliminate things that we are attached to. Whenever you decide to downsize, use the Clutter Remedy strategy to make it as easy and painless as possible. You will want to be emotionally cleared and healed and prepared to move freely, unencumbered by heavy emotions and clutter. It will be astonishing when you see everything you've collected over the years brought into the light and categorized. Feel your feelings, breathe, get lots of rest, and take it slowly. Give yourself plenty of time to complete the process and don't rush.

When Ian, in his late seventies, decided to downsize to an assisted-living apartment, he wanted help figuring out what to keep for the new journey in his life. For years, Ian collected plastic bags and twist ties from the meat and produce section of his local grocery store. He had hundreds of them stuffed into his kitchen. Since they were free, Ian thought he was saving money and that stockpiling them was a smart idea. Every time he went to the store, he would take handfuls of them. When asked what they were for, he replied, "for storing food," yet he had never used any of them. Instead he stored his food in saved glass jars and bottles. He was being a "green" recycler, and what he saved and stored filled his tiny kitchen and spilled onto the countertop. While he considered "free" items as being useful and purposeful, when Ian thought about the seven essential needs (air, food, water, shelter, sleep, elimination, and sunlight), he realized nothing he owned was a "need." He also recognized he had more than a "reasonable" number of free items. Ian symbolized the collection of free items as "thriftiness." His parents had grown up in the Depression and taught him to be thrifty, yet he discovered his "thriftiness" was keeping him from moving forward and purchasing items he really wanted and deserved to have.

Ian had years of memorabilia, mostly photos and papers he was going to keep, and items he would never use again, like tools, office equipment, and really old, tattered furniture he was willing to part with. He struggled with the idea of giving up his things and was saddened by getting older and less active, but he realized certain items did not have a place in his life, and he would have no space for them. He said, "I deserve a new couch, a recliner, and an up-to-date bedroom set and a comfortable, well-made mattress." By focusing on decorating a new space and meeting new friends, Ian had a smooth transition.

Parting with objects that represent our earlier life or former self can be very hard, since we fear losing those memories. Activities like sewing, woodworking, scrapbooking, building, crafts, cooking, exercising, baking, reading, boating, skiing, tennis, and more can represent and define stages of our lives we've long grown past. Even when we know we'll never do those activities again, keeping the stuff keeps the possibility open and reminds us of those active and fun times. Some people keep things with vague plans to give the items to relatives, friends, neighbors, or religious or charity organizations. We think that, surely, someone somewhere will love these items the way we do. When someone wants to keep things in order to give them to others, I always recommend contacting those people; text pictures of the items and ask intended recipients if they want them. If so, great, and if not, a charity will be grateful to take them.

When items kept for sentimental reasons are torn, tattered,

smelly, or just plain gross, I suggest photographing them for memory's sake. Taking a picture of stuffed animals and worn-out objects that you don't want displayed or boxed is a great way to keep the memory without keeping the object, and these photos can be turned into custom-made books and albums. As I discussed earlier (see page 51), when collections of memorabilia are actively treasured, they are ideally displayed or stored in well-labeled, beautiful boxes and containers, to keep the memories reachable, so they don't simply gather dust and take up space.

When downsizing, some people want to keep things that they believe are genuinely valuable. They are convinced these are items that someone will want to inherit or that are worth selling. If so, I suggest they do so: sell them or pass them on. Why wait? However, sentiment often inflates the fair market value of many items. How much is Grandma's cracked china, dated clothing, antique furniture, cookware, and knickknacks worth in today's market? Check with an appraiser or compare similar items for sale online. When people discover saved items are not as valuable as expected, this helps them recognize the real reason they are being saved. Then they can keep them for that reason or donate them. Sometimes certain items simply have symbolic meaning. Symbolizing things as you transition and move helps you get to the real reason things are still in your real estate.

Getting organized to downsize is easier when you realize all the benefits of having a new space, all the things you love, less responsibility, and more fun! Whenever you are on the move, look toward the future rather than the past for a smooth and easy transition.

CLUTTER-FREE CHILDREN'S SPACE

When families use the Clutter Remedy strategy to declutter and organize the entire home, this process will include organizing children and their rooms. Engage the help of each child in categorizing and fine-tuning their things; ask for their ideas and preferences. Then accommodate those ideas and preferences into the organization of their space. Have children identify their values and goals, and include them in planning and the work itself. Of course, depending on their age, children want various levels of assistance, and younger children will not be able to provide too much help with lifting and such. However, all children, except for infants, can be included in and responsible for the organization and care of their own space.

Children want boundaries and rules, and if you don't like the word *rules*, call them guidelines. Preparing them for life helps them feel safe. Teaching kids categorizing and fine-tuning skills and helping them change their language will put them ahead of the game. Help them make good decisions about what to keep and how to set up their space; these are life skills they will use forever.

Educating children about impeding language will help them keep up with their homework and activities, as well as keep their room neat and organized. Helping kids develop an "ideal" friend list, and an "ideal" activity list, helps them think about what they value and dream about. At the end of each summer, creating goals with your kids for the entire school year gives them something to look forward to. Before the beginning of each school year, getting everything spick-and-span is smart, too.

Getting Everything Spick-and-Span

First, organize your thoughts and ideas about what you want for your children's rooms and play space. Then include the kids in the process of emptying their rooms and categorizing everything into bins. Once everything is off the floor and surfaces, have the kids' areas deep-cleaned before putting anything back into their room. Next, use the Clear and Concise Criteria and discard worn-out items like clothing, toys, books, linens, and bedding. Then fine-tune everything and find space-saving organizational storage bins to keep their rooms clutter-free. Large cloth or soft plastic baskets or rubber tubs with handles are great for keeping children's stuffed animals and toys in their bedroom off the floor and the surfaces. Purchase items such as hampers, bins with labels, and decorative boxes to keep things contained and to help kids put their things away.

Schedule a day to teach your children to independently categorize and put things back into their designated homes. Teach them about giving to charity by encouraging them to donate unwanted toys, books, electronics, and knickknacks. Help them part with items that are no longer age-appropriate. You can prepare children to do this for themselves by involving them in the process of organizing their space. Having your children contribute to this process will impede overcollecting and saving behaviors, and it will help your children learn the skills of staying organized for the rest of their lives. I often talk to kids who are defiant about keeping their room organized. They pile toys, clothes, and papers all over their space and avoid putting things away. They are told over and over to stay organized, but they are not always cooperative, and that's where the guidelines and consequences come in handy. Jonny, a single father, reported that when he finds his kids' toys strewn about, he takes the toys away for a limited amount of time, using assertive and validating language. This, he says, "has kept toys where they belong."

Setting boundaries takes parental effort, but your child will appreciate the guidance. Getting them prepared to be organized at home will prepare them for school, college, work, and life in general. Remind your child as they enter their teens that managing their environment is important, especially if they are going to be someone's college roommate someday. Discussing the consequences of clutter and how being organized will affect their future is important, though of course, organizing kids is much easier when you and all other adults in the home are organized and when you know how you want your kids' areas ultimately situated and designed.

When one of the goals is to upgrade your children's rooms, discuss this with them so they are part of the planning. Listen to their ideas about color and design and what colors resonate with them. Engage each child in decorating and organizing their space.

When organizing kids' spaces using the Clutter Remedy strategy, I suggest *not* categorizing younger children's toys. Children play with random toys and choose things to play with to act out what is going on in their lives. Watching them play will tell you a lot about their inner experiences. You want young kids to have an organic way of playing. As they get older, showing them how to separate puzzles from coloring books, and pens from pencils, will be helpful to give them a clear space, but for younger children, teaching them to place their toys into large rubber bins is great to clear the floor and get everything out of the way.

6

REINVENTING AND INVIGORATING YOUR SPACE

When was the last time you took a good look at your space without all the clutter in the way? Do you know what your current "today taste" is? Have you thought of the best way to set up your space so that you can make the best use of it? If not, now is a good time. If you think you are what I call "décor challenged," or you're not into decorating and design, you can learn about design and furniture placement by going online, reading magazines, watching design shows, or hiring a professional. Getting organized and decluttered is the beginning of creating an ideal space. The next step is to create a well-designed space. The better shape your place is in, the more you will be invested in staying organized. Knowing your current taste and preferences for paint color, flooring, furniture, décor, and lighting is not difficult. Nine times out of ten you will know exactly what you love.

FIGURE OUT YOUR "TODAY TASTE"

Figuring out what appeals to you in home design is about getting to know what you love — not like, but love. You could have preferred yellow paint, yet now prefer gray. A neutral look can help you feel safe and calm, but now you want something more edgy and colorful. You could have inherited someone else's taste and never explored your own. You will only know what you love with some insight and exploration. Generally, your taste will change every seven to eight years, without you noticing the shift from one style to another. For instance, with fabric, do you like plaids or solids, stripes or dots, geometrical, silk, velvet, cottons, or chenille? With flooring, do you prefer wood, stone, marble, tile, or laminate? With window coverings, are you drawn to drapes, shutters, or shades? Do you like carpet, rugs, or both?

Whether current trends are interesting or practical for your taste, it is helpful to evaluate them and educate yourself about design options. Will you go with a timeless look or a trend? It is all up to you. Modern or traditional, colonial or Asian, eclectic or farmhouse, craftsman or bungalow, "beachy" and casual or vintage and ornate: Review them all and decide what makes you feel comfortable and cozy, enraptured and stimulated. Consider as many ideas as you can to know what grabs you and takes your breath away. Your taste could still have remained the same and not changed at all for the last forty years, and that is okay, too. The idea is to find what you are comfortable with today and what thrills you.

After clearing up years and years of clutter from Eunice's home, I found her décor extremely dated and old-fashioned. Floral fabric from the early eighties was everywhere, in burgundy and forest green colors. A plaid couch with a dated skirt in those same colors was in her family room. All the furniture was colonial and Victorian, lace was on top of every table, and fake floral arrangements were displayed throughout. There was no sign of any current designs anywhere. I brought up the subject of updating her look, but that *was* Eunice's "today look." She loved what she had. I realized that I wanted to put my ideas of design onto her space, and that was not okay. Don't let anyone helping you with design impose their ideas or keep you from exploring the ideas you love. Taste is a personal preference.

Harry, a successful entrepreneur and retired CPA, had always loved designing and renovating properties. He and his wife, Gabby, usually worked with interior designers on decorating their homes, and they helped them formulate their taste. Harry never thought much about modern design until he was in his eighties. He and Gabby had always chosen a traditional and eclectic look. At eighty-two, Harry woke up one day after a big decluttering and decided he wanted everything to be ultra-modern. He told Gabby they were getting rid of everything they owned from the past forty years. They sold or gave away every stitch of furniture and artwork, and renovated every facet of their home. They bought all new, extremely modern furniture, artwork, flooring, rugs, and décor. The house went from traditional — filled with tchotchkes, classic art, leopard prints, fancy silk couches, gold finishes, and antique pieces — to a very sleek, sparse-looking house with modern art, solid gray and white fabrics, leather and tweed couches, and silver finishes. It screamed minimalism. In the long run, Gabby found it as refreshing as Harry did.

When you live clutter-free, whether you are a minimalist or a maximalist, so many things are possible. When you live in a gorgeous and well-appointed space, it's a lot like living in a luxury hotel suite every day of your life. Once you get a taste of living in an organized and stylized space, you won't ever want to go back.

TIPS FOR INVIGORATING YOUR SPACE

Now that you have gone through the Clutter Remedy strategy — decluttering, categorizing, and fine-tuning — here are some additional ways to create and maintain a lively, clear space, and declutter further. More than merely cleaning and arranging, these are ways to polish your space so that it is inspiring and embodies or reflects positive attributes and ways to live.

- **Keep windows clean:** Just as your eyes are the "windows of the soul," windows are the "eyes of your home." Dirty windows symbolize that your vision is blinded and cloudy, while clean windows represent seeing your potential and opportunities clearly. Keep windows clean so you can always see the literal and metaphorical horizon.

- **Keep the front door clean:** The front door is the first thing people see when they come to your home, and it represents the beginning with you. Energy comes in and out of your doors and windows. When clean, the front door area brings positive energy; when dirty and unattractive, it repels abundance. Put purple flowers near the front door to attract abundance.

- **Replace burned-out lightbulbs and broken lamps:** When lamps and lightbulbs are burned out, it means you are burnt out and cannot see your future prospects. Adequate lighting helps you see a bright and favorable life ahead.

- **Tighten knobs, handles, and bathroom faucets:** Loose handles represent losing your grip. Everything slips away, and you can't hold on to money, friends, family, or anything you're working on.

- **Ensure plants are healthy:** Dead plants represent dead energy. Always have lively, happy, well-fed, and well-watered plants. Fame, recognition, expansion, financial prosperity, and health depend on healthy living things in your home and office.

- **Keep toilet lids down and drains covered:** Leave toilet seats and lids down and cover drains in order to protect your energy (or chi) from going down the drain, along with your wealth, knowledge, health, and other valuables. In addition, close the door to all bathrooms when you leave.

- **Store nothing under the bed:** Symbolically, storing items of any kind under the bed represents underlying issues you cannot sort through. Stuffing items under the bed hinders your dream state and waking life, and it makes for restless sleep. For a peaceful slumber, keep the area under the bed clear and dust-free.

- **Keep mirrors clean:** When mirrors are dirty, you cannot see yourself clearly, and that makes it impossible for anyone else to see you clearly. Plus, like my mother always said when she would see someone who looked disheveled walking down the street, "Did they look in the mirror this morning?" Mirrors help keep you polished and attractive. When mirrors are sprayed with toothpaste and dirt, you cannot attract what you desire in life, and you will miss out on clear opportunities, people, and self-understanding.

- **Store nothing behind doors:** When you store any items, such as mirrors or pictures, behind a door, it means you have a hidden agenda. Items blocking any part of the door represent blocked opportunities. To expand your options, remove anything that keeps doors from opening and closing completely and without hindrance.

- **Fix drips and leaks:** Leaking water represents leaking wealth; fix leaks to keep money from draining out of your life.

- **Sharpen pencils and dispose of old, nonworking pens and markers.** They represent a nonworking part of you.

- **In closets, arrange clothes on hangers with the front of the clothes all going in the same direction:** Replace all bulky wooden, wire, and plastic hangers with slim hangers. Having all the hangers match helps keep your clothes from becoming disarrayed. This is symbolic of creating a more harmonious lifestyle.

- **Remove all fake flowers, silk plants, dried flowers, fake fruit, and replicas of living things:** These are dust collectors that "suck" energy from you and your dwelling. Symbolically, these represent fake aspects of yourself! At minimum, keep the "fake" stuff clean and dust-free.

- **Regularly clear your computer and devices of spam and negative information:** Regularly seeing negative information causes unease and anxiety. In general, do what you can to decrease the amount of junk email and solicitations you receive. If your work involves dealing with problems, complaints, and "ugly" information, develop a system to keep only positive information on your computer. Transfer negative information onto backup devices.

- **Regularly clear out your refrigerator and pantry:** Similarly, make a habit of disposing of old, expired food and any other food items that are no longer edible. Clean refrigerator and pantry shelves regularly.

- **Clean out purses and briefcases regularly:** Make sure you have a home for receipts, business cards, and notes, and throw away wrappers and trash from purses and briefcases. Clean the outside of purses and briefcases daily with a spray solution and cloth, since these collect bacteria.

- **Continually declutter:** Clutter in your home, or keeping items you don't use or cherish, symbolizes holding on to negativity and not making room for new opportunities. Throw unwanted things away or put them in the garage and regularly donate them to charity.

- **Avoid art and objects that make you sad:** Representations of death, people drinking, drug use, tragedy (including people who died tragically, like Marilyn Monroe and Elvis), and sad characters symbolically bring that into your realm. Art depicting hunting, ferocious animals, and war symbolically brings violence and hatred into your heart and home. In addition, avoid art that depicts only one of something, like a single bird or flower; this represents feeling or being alone.

ARRANGE ROOMS TO MANIFEST HAPPINESS AND PROSPERITY

Like the saying "open sesame," unobstructed space and well-designed furniture and décor placement will create a free means of access, admission, and sparkle to every room. Creating good energy and flow instantly makes a room intriguing and enchanting, but it does more than that. How living spaces are arranged will help you relax and become more creative in manifesting your goals. When you think that something is blocking you from reaching your goals, review your space and notice anything blocking the pathways. Consider rearranging tightly spaced furniture that blocks the energy of each room. For instance, facing furniture toward the room's entrance avoids a closed or boxed-in feeling and keeps the room open and inviting — both literally and metaphorically. How furniture in your space is set up affects your emotions and health and influences what you bring into your life.

For example, Michelle had been in great health when she decided to move closer to her grandkids, but shortly after moving, she felt fatigued, boxed in, and dreadful. When I arrived, the first thing I noticed was that her couch faced the fireplace and the television, with its back to the entrance of the room. To sit down, you walked around the entire couch. Michelle explained that she felt uneasy sitting on the couch, as if something would "surprise" her from behind.

To solve this, we rearranged the furniture so the couch faced the opening of the room, creating an open and welcoming space. Of course, this change required moving the rest of her furniture, including artwork and the television. Michelle hired a handyman to move the flat-screen television and to rewire, patch, and paint. Next, we worked on decluttering and moving things around in her kitchen. After, she was amazed at how her mood and energy were back to normal. When I followed up with Michelle a year later, she was excited to tell me that she was "healthy and settled" and she had "slimmed down over twenty pounds" by eliminating certain unhealthy foods.

Beverly had been single for a long time. When I assessed her home, I noticed only one nightstand. We added another one, not only for balance, but to symbolize bringing a partner into her life. She also decluttered items that made her sad and guilty and that did not meet her criteria for keeping around. After the change, she noticed that she was more balanced, and she started to date a guy who met her criteria for an ideal partner. She reported feeling "more fulfilled than ever before." After Phoebe rearranged her kids' rooms, family room, and garage, she told me that she felt anxiety-free and at peace for the first time in years.

Trent was a successful businessman. He had money pouring in, yet he had been divorced and single for eight years, with no love in sight. First, Trent and I discussed what he valued in life. He told me he wanted to find a partner. His goal was to meet someone within the next year and get married again. He was missing love and felt confused and desperate much of the time. I noticed that his backyard — where he enjoyed gardening, entertaining, and hanging out — lacked a sitting area. So we placed a gazebo in the backyard to create an area for friends to gather, with the intention of bringing some love into his life. We decorated the gazebo with bungalow furniture that matched the architecture of his home, along with red and purple pillows, cushions, candles, and artwork that symbolized "love" to Trent. The gazebo inspired Trent with the exciting possibilities of romance, and within one year, he met the love of his life.

Making simple changes to your space with the intention of bringing your dreams to life can help increase your motivation, creativity, and wealth. It can facilitate career changes and a better social life and love life. Moving furniture apart gives rooms a more "airy" feeling; creating open walkways helps you breathe, sleep, and live more easily in your space. Your space's energy has the potential to stimulate creativity and inspiration.

Decorate and fill your space with objects that symbolize your ideal lifestyle. Figure out how and where to place objects so they don't look clumped together, such as by categorizing and displaying things in cases. Deliberately placing objects and fixing up empty spaces can enhance your life and fill your lifestyle with everything you've dreamed about.

RENOVATING AND BEAUTIFYING YOUR SPACE

The extent to which you renovate, redecorate, or redesign your space depends on your budget, energy, and time. Depending on your level of experience, renovating a space will feel exciting, terrifying, or both. Either way, it's a big commitment, and it usually requires hiring professionals to do some or all of the work. Nevertheless, your goals and choices drive the work, since it's your ideal home or workspace you are creating. If you're going to do a thorough remodel, consider taking an interior design class to give you ideas and help with planning. Here is a quick overview of things to keep in mind.

Hiring Contractors

When you have a large, complex project, a good way to find a contractor that you like is to hire them for a small part of the project and see how they are to work with. In general, when looking for contractors, get referrals from neighbors and from online neighborhood venues. Then do your research, check online reviews, and call recent references. I once checked the references for a flooring guy without realizing they were from years ago. I'm sure he'd been an excellent contractor in the past, but he made blunder after blunder in my home, and eventually he admitted he had recently lost his wife, relapsed, and was not motivated to work.

During the work itself, be on-site at all times, or have someone who knows design help keep a close watch on the quality of the work. Contractors and workers don't want someone breathing down their neck, but when homeowners aren't around, they can get lax. Contractors often leave their workers unsupervised, so poke your nose into your masterpiece anytime you want. Speak up if you see something that bothers you or that you know is off. Remember, it's your space and your money, and you are the "boss."

Renovation Considerations

Renovating, decorating, and designing a space can be overwhelming, and sometimes you will think you're going mad, but in good time it's the next step for creating a nirvana home or workspace, and you deserve it.

Decide for yourself how much of this work to do yourself and when to hire professionals. When these improvements require investments of time and money, how much you spend is up to you. Even with a minimal budget, you can accomplish a lot with plenty of dedication and elbow grease.

Whether you want a new coat of paint or an entirely new interior, the goal is to create a space that supports your values and life goals. Creating good energy and flow in your home is more than rearranging furniture. To create an ideal living space, consider paint, wall coverings, flooring, and new furniture that ideally align with your "today taste," and the architecture of your home.

Search for and find furniture that is aesthetically pleasing, practical, and functional. Find furnishings, paintings, and décor at consignment stores and online, or at local furniture makers' studios. Most top designers now are shopping green and finding lightly or barely used high-end pieces that are unique. You can find expensive, quality pieces by shopping green. As long as what you buy is real wood and high quality, you will be happier than if you buy cheap, trendy, "good-looking" pieces.

When you want new items, hire an interior designer to help you find pieces that are made well and that will impress rather than stress you and your bank account. Designers get deep discounts at all the large stores and from manufacturers. Find a designer who will pass these savings on to you.

When you take a good look around your place, you will find that some of your space's contents are misplaced, broken, chipped, and dodgy looking, so continue to declutter. Some of your items could use a coat of paint, or they are no longer "you." Creating ideal space means moving things around and around until a space feels open and wondrous. Like moving clothes with the seasons, I call this dance "musical stuff."

7

HITTING A WALL

Overcollecting, Grief, and
Other Major Obstacles and Barriers

When you are in the process of getting organized and you find yourself stuck and hitting a wall, I want you to understand the obstacles and barriers that could be blocking you from going forward. Becoming overwhelmed by the scope of the job or the process of decluttering can trigger unexpected, strong emotions.

You can become resistant during the decluttering process. This is natural and normal. Clutter arises for a reason, and addressing that reason is part of the process. When you start to declutter during a major life transition, distractions and disruptions can add to the process. Typically, anything disruptive puts getting organized on the back burner. Exhaustion, sadness, divorce, anxiety, work demands, and other priorities can become the center of someone's attention instead of decluttering.

Always be patient with yourself. Don't be too hard on yourself over any mess that's built up or over how long the decluttering process is taking, especially when challenges are present. Mounds of clutter don't happen overnight and are rarely resolved over a weekend. There is a correct time and place for starting the project, and the adventure of organizing is worth it.

However, it's helpful and important to recognize when "normal" resistance, distractions, and mixed emotions are something more serious. Organizing large piles that are blocking you or a loved one from living the life you deserve is not always straightforward. Many challenges will put up a big red stop sign and not allow you to trailblaze your way to becoming and staying perpetually organized. Barriers include health challenges, grief and loss, family dynamics, and having an overly intense relationship with your stuff.

This chapter helps you identify some of the more difficult roadblocks that will undermine an organizing project, and it provides suggestions for coping with them. When the blocks to getting organized are things like mental or physical health challenges, get additional support from loved ones and family and consider hiring a Clutter Remedy organizer to handle the decluttering and organizing project. Pausing the process and addressing the issues that are coming up with a life coach or mental health professional will be helpful when you become derailed.

You deserve to live a life of grandeur, a carefree life even when you want to keep all the things you love. Even a mild amount of clutter can be stifling and overwhelming, but when there is an enormous amount of stuff to declutter, or you experience significant barriers to getting organized, doing it completely on your own will prove difficult. People are often surprised by their experience during this process: For some, it's like a hike up Mount Everest, and for some, it's shockingly easy, like breathing in a soft, warm, wet, salty breeze during a summer holiday. Yet the goal is the same: to create a simpler, more-effectual lifestyle.

Transitioning from disorganized to organized is different for everyone. You and only you will decide when and how to do it. You and only you know when you are ready to begin. Approach your project with enthusiasm and energy, by focusing on your values and goals, and recognize when heavy emotions or conflicts run high. When they do, get help and work through them to keep you on track. You deserve to have an amazing experience as you figure out all that you love about yourself and your stuff.

SIGNS OF MAJOR OBSTACLES AND BARRIERS

It's very easy to become distracted while decluttering and organizing. Picking up a sentimental object can transport you into long-lost memories. You can start to feel unexpected waves of sadness and recall times when you felt regret or longing. Getting overwhelmed and swamped with hundreds of details that pull you in many directions will quickly defeat the process. You will lose focus as you multitask and get bogged down in mental to-do lists. While clearing out junk mail and setting aside bills, financial worries can press one to suddenly review taxes, due dates, and deadlines. There are always more pertinent, pressing matters than organizing your scissors. For a million reasons, it's easy to lose sight of the clutter and start to focus on specific tasks that you have overlooked for years. Past unfinished business and emotional clutter is clearly a deterrent to fixing actual clutter, and when this happens, review "Clearing and Healing Strategy" (see pages 26–28) and use the techniques designed to release negative emotions. However, there are also telltale signs of more serious issues at work or of challenges that, without adequate support, can entirely block a successful organizing project. Here are some of the symptoms to be alert for:

- Intense stress that personal objects will be touched or ruined by others
- Inability to release anything at all, even when items do not meet the Clear and Concise Criteria
- Fatigue and decreased motivation
- Overthinking and overplanning and not being able to start the project
- Increasing anxiety or confusion until the point of the project is lost
- Inability to focus and stay focused on even the smallest task
- Difficulty expressing feelings
- A sense of hopelessness and powerlessness
- Increasing indignant anger when items are moved
- Continually fighting with helpers and/or blaming others for the mess
- Feeling disconnected from helpers and numb to the process of getting organized
- Forgetfulness, confusion, and feeling completely overwhelmed
- Pain, emotional and physical
- Feeling too burdened by taking care of others, whether kids, pets, family, or loved ones

When any of these come up for you, consider getting help so that you will be able to continue decluttering. In many cases, it's possible to cope with these symptoms with the correct support and insight and finish the organizing project. In essence, this involves some combination of practicing better self-care and setting boundaries with others, but the most important first step is recognizing and acknowledging what is going on with yourself and your situation.

Taking the Path of Least Resistance
and Better Self-Care

I often suggest that clients take the path of least resistance when difficult obstacles and barriers surface. This can be the smarter way to reach your organizing goals than wrestling directly with entrenched problems. This doesn't mean "taking the easy way out" or avoiding problems entirely. Rather, look for the fastest, easiest way to accomplish what you want, while minimizing hassle and diversions. Consider the challenge like you would an uncompromising, unreasonable person; rather than remain stuck arguing with them, find a more harmonious and clearer path to reach your goal.

At the same time, pay attention to your health and energy. When you are well-rested, well-fed, and fit, you will think more clearly and have more emotional resilience. Good physical health improves your mental and emotional health, so that you will feel energized, balanced, focused, and elated. Good health improves your motivation and level of attention, both of which are vital to becoming organized. Sometimes, the best medicine is a good night's sleep, proper nutrition, and taking the decluttering process at a good pace, so you avoid exhaustion.

Setting Clear Guidelines and
Boundaries with Others

When you have difficulties with any part of the organizing process, or with people involved in your life, I recommend setting up rules or boundaries for the process. This is no different than setting up rules or guidelines in any relationship that encounters difficulties. While avoiding accusations and blame, clarify boundaries for the space and each person's responsibilities. When particular people within a household won't cooperate or compromise, exclude those people and "their space" from your organizing efforts. Keep concentrating on your stuff, and use the strategies to keep you focused on only what you want to accomplish.

When you haven't set clear boundaries in the past, starting to do this midway into an organizing project will be difficult. I suggest thinking about how you will approach difficult challenges with the people you live or work with from the beginning of the organizing process; see "Resolving Conflicts: Assertive Language and Validation Tool" (pages 42–45). When you don't prepare yourself ahead of time, it will be hard to say no or to set up consequences and then follow through when rules are broken. When there are opposing forces and opinions of how a household is set up and run, the household's clutter is likely an expression or a symbol of dysfunction within the relationship of the people who are at odds. Occasionally, people come to realize that "decluttering the house" is an unconscious attempt to fix a troubled relationship, and sadly, in extreme cases, the only real solution is to get professional help. When that does not work out, it can be best to leave the relationship, smartly and safely, as a form of self-preservation.

Finally, when people feel blamed or judged by others, I recommend a "blue light" visualization: Surround yourself with blue light and send love toward harmful, angry people. The blue light blocks the negativity of others and protects you, as does sending out strong feelings of unconditional love. This blocks the negative energy of others and sends it back to them. Love is more powerful than any type of negative energy. When a lot of love is swirling around hostile people, they generally retreat.

RECORD AND REFLECT ON YOUR DREAMS

Addressing your dreams is an important part of staying perpetually organized. Why? Because our unconscious processes play out in our dreams. The unconscious process is the dark pool of everything that has ever happened to us, which becomes light in our dreams, so we can visit all the experiences that have shaped our life. Dreams reveal things that have occurred in life in a symbolic way, and in symbolic meaning, they will shed light or understanding on difficult issues that come up during decluttering. Remember, the outer is a reflection of the inner self.

Insight into your dreams will reveal blocks or barriers to becoming organized. In the dream state, you will find innovative and fresh ideas. Take time when you wake to reflect on your dreams. Do they contain any insight or information? It is a great practice to keep a dream journal by your bed, so you immediately jot down what you remember, as dreams are quickly forgotten. Many people complain that they do not remember their dreams, but all it takes is intention and practice. Each morning recall whatever bits and pieces you can. Then, prior to going to bed, tell yourself to remember your dreams.

While dreaming, your unconscious process brings into view people, animals, cars, places, dwellings, objects, and images to represent and help you figure out life challenges. Many parts of your child, adolescent, and adult selves will come forth, but remember, everything that comes into the dream state is an aspect of you and what you're wanting to resolve in everyday life.

A dream of a child can be symbolic of childhood events that you have not worked through, or the child could represent a childlike outlook on your current situation. You can have disturbing dreams that symbolize clutter or not fulfilling responsibilities.

When you dream about masculine or feminine figures, they are symbols of the masculine or feminine aspects of yourself. A dream of a male figure fighting with his boss, when you are a woman, can mean that you are struggling with career demands and being a breadwinner.

Whoever and whatever show up are symbolic aspects that

want to be addressed, and it is important to use the clearing and healing exercise (see pages 26–28) to heal those issues or aspects that will block you from getting organized.

Decide for yourself what the content of the dreams symbolizes. As an example, though, if you dream of a whale swallowing you, ponder what that whale represents or symbolizes. The whale can represent a big problem at work, a bossy parent, or a home drowning in debt. Or the whale could be symbolic of the clutter-clustered corners that have formed throughout your home. If you dream of a fish with wings, carrying a house on its back, what does that image mean to you symbolically? Literally, the fish is a fish and a house is a house and wings are wings. Symbolically, it could mean you are uplifting a home that is drowning in clutter, or it could symbolize a flight of ideas and solutions for change and movement in your life. Again, only you will correctly interpret the meaning of your dreams, since the symbols relate to only you and your life.

That said, dream images can be obscure. Allow yourself time to contemplate the symbols until you identify meaningful connections to the challenges in your life, and when the challenges continue to block you, consider getting help from a Clutter Remedy expert for your decluttering project.

FRIENDLY VISITORS: HIRING A PROFESSIONAL ORGANIZER

When you encounter challenges starting or finishing a decluttering project, consider hiring a professional organizer familiar with the Clutter Remedy strategy. They can be helpful in any circumstance, but especially when someone is struggling with physical, emotional, mental, or practical challenges that make organizing difficult, if not impossible. The focus of professional organizers is to improve people's lives.

The profession is similar to the early 1800s' "friendly visitors" program. Friendly visitors helped people get through rough times and provided care and support when a family or community could not. A friendly visitor arrived with a fruit basket on their arm, offering warm and kind words. They put their organizational skills to work keeping order and maintaining calm. The visitor would be called when a woman had let the house go due to being pregnant or having to go back to work. They would visit when an elderly person had lost their strength and couldn't put away groceries or organize the mail. They were there to help a man who lost his wife or a family who lost their breadwinner and had no one to manage the household. When people suffered from grief and loss, physical disability, and other overwhelming life transitions, friendly visitors would attend to the nitty-gritty details of life and keep the ball rolling: doing the laundry, cleaning out the pantry, and straightening up the home.

Trained and experienced professional organizers are today's "friendly visitors." With clarity and vision, they will help when you are experiencing any physical or emotional challenges, grief or loss, or are overwhelmed with other responsibilities. Carefully evaluate the person you are considering hiring, as you would when hiring any contractor or professional to work on your house. Some people call themselves "professional organizers" without having any particular background or experience. I recommend looking for someone who has owned and operated an organizing business for a minimum of five years and who is a member of an organization offering organizer support and education. In addition, you will want them to have expertise or experience in space design and know the Clutter Remedy strategy.

Meet or talk with someone before hiring them and get a sense for their personality. You want to hire someone you feel comfortable working with, whatever their expertise. To me, the most important traits to look for are kindness and empathy, a nonjudgmental attitude, good communication skills, a positive demeanor, and a goal-oriented focus. You want someone who is flexible, creative, and adaptable, especially when there are more serious mental health challenges such as overcollecting and over-accumulation.

OVERCOLLECTING AND OVERSHOPPING

Over time, many people develop "collections" that represent their enthusiasms or sense of identity. These sentimental, loved items will or will not still support their lives and be worth keeping, but addressing collections is a common aspect of the decluttering process. However, some people become obsessed with collecting, or they are addicted to shopping, to an extent that is self-defeating. The urge to acquire and save becomes an extreme behavior that disrupts the person's normal life, and it will not be solved by getting organized. Someone who overcollects can feel threatened by the decluttering process and refuse to go along or participate.

In addition, people who collect obsessively often can't explain why they do it. I once encountered a man who over the course of fifty years collected thousands of egg cartons. He symbolized the egg cartons as "possibly useful," but this gentleman died before he ever figured out a use for them. I've met with people who filled their entire homes with collections of crafts, fabrics, milk cartons, and old newspapers. When I ask, "Why milk cartons?" or "Why newspapers?" the answer is often simply "because." In these cases, the reasons usually have nothing to do with the items being collected. Instead, the person is filling an emotional hole with stuff.

One example of shopping addiction was Rhonda, an owner of a large corporation. She loved to buy office and food products in bulk, far more than could be used before the expiration dates, and she loved to buy holiday items and congratulatory items for special occasions and every season. I was called by the office manager, who was in charge of the storage rooms and keeping things organized. By this time, the products Rhonda continually ordered were spilling into hallways, blocking floors, and filling every unoccupied cubicle. Rhonda was not interested in any of the solutions I offered. I suggested redesigning the storage areas and adding new shelving to organize all the products and holiday items, but she remarked that it was "too expensive." I suggested donating or selling some of the items, but Rhonda did neither. Instead, Rhonda's solution was to get a larger office space and rent off-site storage for the holiday items. Clearly, no storage solution was going to solve Rhonda's shopping habits. Her inability to pare down and stop spending and overcollecting ultimately destroyed the business. Her manager found another job, and Rhonda eventually went bankrupt.

When a loved one suffers from overcollecting, their family often hopes that decluttering will be the solution that helps them improve their lives. But it isn't that simple. In extreme cases, I recommend a gentle approach. People can't be forced to give up maladaptive coping behaviors too quickly, and sometimes the only lasting solution will be to seek professional help. However, when organizing is welcomed by the person, I say, "Let's see how it goes, and then we'll make a plan."

Finding more space, building more shelves, and organizing won't solve overspending and overcollecting. These behaviors are compensating for emotional challenges or perhaps past trauma. The "hole" that people are wanting to fill with things can be caused by low self-esteem, loss, shame, pain, doubt, regret, loneliness, or even boredom. There can be a lack of connection to others, a poor support system, or a disconnection with their inner self. Whatever the reasons, this sense of emptiness cannot be filled by stuff, nor will it be fixed by simply decluttering their things.

It can be more effective to approach overcollecting and

overshopping the same way addictions are treated. Lasting solutions depend on changing one's lifestyle: getting enough rest and sleep, eating well, having meaningful work and a sense of purpose, and developing supportive relationships. When someone figures out how to be self-fulfilled and feel positive about life, the urge to collect decreases, and they understand that stuff, products, and belongings are not a sign of health or happiness. Matter matters, but not at the expense of breaking the bank or your spirit.

Organizing Collections for People Not Willing to Purge

Of course, overcollecting, overshopping, and overaccumulating can create unsafe, unlivable, and often deadly environments. Everyone, even the person who is doing the collecting, will recognize that change is a good idea, and how much change will vary for each person.

Those who remain highly attached to every single item can toy with the idea of change yet not want to part with one thing, and that's okay. They want to keep everything, even wrappers and popsicle sticks, and any attempt to throw anything away will result in a futile, upsetting tug-of-war that causes harm and stress for everyone.

In these extreme situations, my approach is to honor the person's belongings, their feelings, and the effort it took to collect them, while promising not to get rid of anything. Instead, by slightly modifying the Clutter Remedy strategy in chapter 3, I suggest simply categorizing, fine-tuning, and containing the collection. Restoring a livable home is the goal. We still clear the entire contents out of the existing space and go through the same broad/fine-tuning/containing strategy — where every single object in the home ends up with like objects — yet no editing or purging is involved. Then we create a clear and organized space by putting all categorized items into clear plastic bins, and placing those bins out of walkways and off the furniture, preferably on shelving. If shelving is not an option, then the bins can be stacked anywhere where they are safe and in clear view.

This approach has been successful, since the person gets to keep all their stuff, and they can see and access their belongings with clarity. This simmers down collecting and churning behaviors. *Churning* is the process of obsessively going through piles and piles of stuff, over and over, moving stuff around and reconfiguring piles, then digging through the mounds again frequently. People find that keeping categorized items in clear bins, so they are visible and close by, is comforting; everything is accounted for and easy to access. To their own amazement, people discover that their lives will become clutter-free, while keeping all of their precious belongings, and they can reclaim a safe and orderly space.

For instance, Dina collected everything and anything that she could find in alleyways, dumpsters, thrift stores, and online. This behavior had gained momentum ten years before, when her husband filed for divorce, and she had a split with her children because of her extreme overcollecting behaviors. Dina's kids thought putting a boundary up with her behaviors would push her to get some help, and when she didn't, they continued to stay away from her. Dina told me that she had been "abandoned" by her family. She collected things that symbolized being a "good wife" and a "good mom." She collected household and kitchen items, cleaning products, foil and plastic zipped bags, aprons, office supplies, ironing boards and irons, food products, and books. Dina had over six hundred books, mostly on parenting, relationships, crafts, cooking, gardening, organizing, and decorating.

Dina did not have insight into what would be a reasonable amount to keep, and she had avoided the idea of getting organized. In past attempts at getting organized, Dina reported having bouts of depression and volatile anger toward anyone who talked about getting rid of stuff. My approach appealed to her: I established a "no get rid of" policy and expressed my philosophy of having respect for each individual and their autonomy. I promised that, without forcing her to do anything she didn't want, we could safely and effectively design her space. So she let me and my team in, and after we were done, Dina couldn't believe her eyes. She cried so hard that she shook. It was a cathartic moment, and we cried with her.

Dina was so grateful and astonished that she could keep, see, and have access to every little scrap she owned. She was excited to have her pathway back and to sit on her couch and sleep in her bed again. She expressed relief that her kids and friends would return to her life, which they did once they understood more about her. The reasons for Dina's behavior were complex and serious: She had been abused and abandoned emotionally in her childhood, and a fire had burned down her home when she was seven years old, destroying all that she cherished — her stuffed animals, dolls, and toys, all that had been her only comforts in her young life. Dina was able to open up and share a great deal about herself and her desire to love her children and be a part of their lives, but that did not change how she thought about her stuff.

Dina liked to follow the rules and guidelines that we gave her for managing her things. She understood that if she took something out of a bin, she would will herself to put it back when she was finished with it. She recognized categorizing, fine-tuning, and containing as an easy way to stay organized. It was a safer way to live, and for someone with her amount of stuff, it allowed her home to be set up in a more "normal" way. The important lesson is that it is not anyone's place to tell people what they can and can't keep in their space and their life. I say, "No matter the matter, it's on me, as the organizer, to set it all up properly." Also, when organizing any space, no matter how much or little there is, it will always be easier when your physical health is good, and your goal is to have a healthier lifestyle.

PHYSICAL CHALLENGES AND A HEALTHY LIFESTYLE

Decluttering can be physically challenging. It's a workout. In extreme cases, people will struggle to maintain the stamina to finish the project. In essence, their own lack of health stops them from improving their life.

If this happens, one solution is to get help: Ask friends and family to assist you, or hire a professional organizer who uses the Clutter Remedy strategy. Another solution is to give yourself more time to complete the process, so you don't become exhausted. However, long-term, improving your health requires changing your behavior and adjusting diet and exercise. Protecting and caring for your body will help you meet any other challenges you face. You can equate great health habits with great organizing habits.

Healthy Lifestyle Tips

- **Exercise daily:** Exercise increases energy and a feeling of well-being. It is great for your cardiovascular and mental health. Yoga, walking, biking, and swimming are great exercises that are easy on the body.
- **Avoid unhealthy foods:** Avoid eating foods high in saturated and trans fats, fatty meats, table salt, too much dairy, and sweets. Harsh vinegars, sodas, and chemicals in food are especially harmful to the body and the mind. You can find you are intolerant of certain foods, such as dairy, wheat, or nuts. Experiment

with eliminating particular foods until you feel healthy, and get a regularly scheduled checkup.

- **Get adequate sleep:** If you don't sleep well, find out why. Consult with a physician, or perhaps take a natural herbal sleep product. Good sleep is achieved through a fixed sleep schedule and by avoiding eating food, using electronics, and intensely exercising before bed. Also, avoid caffeinated beverages in the afternoon and evening.
- **Socialize:** Going out with friends and joining groups keeps you active. Go dancing or to movies, learn how to golf, or join a book club.
- **Walk in nature:** We *need* adequate sunlight, and nature is refreshing mentally and emotionally. Walking on cool sand or picking wildflowers is grounding and stimulates the senses.

Finally, improve your health as you declutter and organize. Go through your pantry and refrigerator and read all the ingredients of your food products, and eliminate products with hydrogenated oils, dyes, corn syrup, preservatives, corn starch, and anything you know is not good for you. Read the labels of everything you consume. You are what you eat. When you can't understand the ingredients on the labels, it's time to do some research. Eat fresh, whole, organic foods and include a lot of fresh vegetables and fruit. Make a point of improving your diet. When people complain about poor health, sometimes the culprit is in their pantry.

Your diet and health can affect you emotionally. Watch for anything that triggers you during the process of getting organized, and incorporate better eating habits and helpful coping strategies.

GETTING TRIGGERED: WORKING THROUGH INTENSE EMOTIONS

As I've mentioned, decluttering can trigger intense emotions. People will sometimes get so upset and worked up in the middle of the process that they can't continue, leaving themselves with an even bigger mess on their hands. In addition, unresolved, underlying emotional issues are a primary cause of backsliding, or finding that clutter returns and someone can't sustain perpetual organization due to unmanaged health challenges. Negative emotions affect our ability to care for ourselves, others, and our environment, so it's no surprise they can deter our success at decluttering.

Emotional issues are not caused by the decluttering process. Instead, facing clutter can bring them up, leading to what I call an "irritable mood syndrome." Some people get on an emotional roller coaster, so that their mood swings wildly day to day, even hour to hour. Everyone experiences mood shifts, but most of the time we adjust back to a balanced state fairly quickly. However, if you experience extreme mood swings — like shifting rapidly between tears and exhilaration — or find that dark moods can last for days or even weeks, this can signal a more serious condition to address.

Consider what is causing the irritability and moodiness. There are many potential factors, such as medications you're taking, poor sleep, poor diet, lack of exercise, a hormone imbalance, or an alcohol or drug problem. It could be a psychological issue, like trauma, abuse, or poor self-esteem. Even the environment can be a factor. Here are some questions to help figure out what could be triggering perpetual moodiness:

1. Have you had aggressive relationships that scarred you?
2. Have you experienced a trauma?

3. Were you exposed to toxins in the environment?
4. Have you lost someone you loved, including a pet?
5. Do you have unresolved grief and loss?
6. Did you take a blow to the head or get into an accident?
7. Have you been in a war?
8. Are you going through a change of life or lifestyle?

To address trauma and unresolved emotions, the best step is to meet with a qualified medical and mental health practitioner. These types of professionals can diagnose the issue and suggest the appropriate ways to deal with it, whether through talk therapy, support groups, lifestyle changes, natural or nonaddictive medications, or all of the above. Organizing stuff doesn't fix negative emotions. That said, below are four suggestions for coping in everyday ways with emotional struggles.

Four Strategies for Managing Negative Thoughts and Emotions

Depending on your situation, these four strategies will help when negative thoughts and emotions threaten to derail the organizing process.

Shoulder tapping validation: Every time you have negative thoughts and make a negative statement about yourself, tap yourself on the shoulder, tell yourself to stop, and then say the opposite of the negative statement. For example, if you caught yourself thinking or saying, "I'm stupid, I'm disorganized, I'm messy, and I can't cope," physically tap your own shoulder and say, "Stop that," your name, and then, "I'm smart, I'm organized, I'm very neat, and I cope well." It doesn't matter if you believe these affirmative statements at first. Say them anyway; this strategy works by instilling positive self-statements into your subconscious process. By practicing this regularly, you will become more confident, self-aware, and protective of yourself and your stuff.

Rope and anchor visualization: When you fall into a less desirable mood, envision a strong rope pulling you into a more pleasant thought. If you feel lofty, out of touch, and disconnected from yourself or others, visualize an anchor coming out of your heart center and anchoring into the ground below you. Imaginatively stabilizing yourself when you feel unbalanced and crazed keeps you focused on the goal of getting organized.

Practice adaptive coping skills: In the past, such as in childhood, how did you cope with aggravation and disappointment? Return to any healthy, positive coping strategies that you've used before to find comfort and restore a positive, constructive outlook. This can include coloring and drawing, being alone and contemplating, hanging out with friends, writing poetry, playing darts or sports, or reading a book. Sometimes we forget about coping strategies that have worked in the past, and most likely they will still work now.

Create an ideal lifestyle dream board: Begin by visualizing your own ideal lifestyle. Next, cut out pictures, words, and symbols from magazines and advertisements — or print online images — that represent your ideal lifestyle. Collect anything that winks and twinkles at you. Then place the images on a large piece of posterboard, creating a dream board that evokes and awakens your ideal lifestyle. You can do a dream board of your ideal career, an ideal business, an ideal home, an ideal partnership, or whatever you want to bring into your life. The board is a representation and reminder of what you truly stand for and believe about life, and this can help focus and inspire you as you clear your space and arrange your stuff.

COPING WITH GRIEF AND LOSS

Disorganization will follow devastation. When a loved one dies, it is hard to get up in the morning, much less clean the kitchen, do laundry, mow the lawn, and make a healthy dinner. Clearing out a loved one's stuff can be hardest of all, since it represents the person you lost and moving forward without them, and it can trigger people to confront their loss. The passage of time will not make this task any easier. The pain of losing a loved one — whether a cherished person or pet, and whether the loss is from death, divorce, or deception — can remain for a long time, even after people think they have recovered. Then, when those feelings return, people become devastated and lifeless all over again, with no motivation to thrive and prosper.

Brandy told me that when her husband passed away she stopped functioning altogether. She stopped cleaning, going out, and even bathing. She stopped gardening, watching films, reading, and cooking. Clutter piled up to the point that she was sleeping on the couch for months. Death or loss knocks some people to the ground, and everyone has a different time frame as to when they feel some semblance of happiness and balance. As a former psychotherapist, I was frequently asked, "When will the pain go away?" There is no correct answer, since everyone is different in how they process grief.

I once knew someone who lost a beloved turtle and did not recover from their grief for decades. Conversely, I've known men and women who lost their partners after fifty years of marriage and then remarried within six months. You can't predict how long grieving will take. There is no time limit on how long it will take to grieve. The key is to grieve well and for as long as it takes.

Human beings, in general, are very uncomfortable with grief. We are told or expect ourselves to "get over it," and then "it" becomes an unresolved issue. One way or another, when grieving, you want to go through the five stages of grief or loss: denial, anger, bargaining, depression, and acceptance. These were devised by Elisabeth Kübler-Ross in her book *On Death and Dying*. She eventually came to doubt and deny her own theory when she herself was dying, but the stages are correct, and they also do not go in sequence. Many people start off with denial, but I have seen people jump immediately to anger, bargaining, or depression. Depression seems to be the stage most people attempt to avoid. They bounce between denial, bargaining, and anger for years to avoid the stage of depression, which is the doorway back to high functioning.

The greatest example of denial I've experienced was a ninety-year-old woman named Maria. I met her over twenty years ago when I was a home health social worker. I was given the assignment to check in on her by her home health nurse. When I arrived, I noticed a giant painting of her husband on the wall and a bearskin rug on the floor. She proceeded to tell me all about her husband and how he was a "bear hunter." As Maria went on and on, I noticed a pipe on her living room table, a man's hat on the side of the chair, and other masculine objects throughout the home. Eventually, as I was getting ready to leave, I asked Maria when her husband would be home. Maria turned pale as a ghost and shrieked, "My husband has been dead for over thirty years!" I jumped out of my skin in shock. Given the contents of the home and her stories about him, I assumed her husband was very much alive and living with her and that he would walk through the door at any moment. We scared each other that night! I told her how sorry I was and then, embarrassed, shuffled off to my car.

Only afterward was I told by her nurse: Maria lived alone and would normally "retaliate in furious denial when confronted with her husband's passing." Somehow, my ignorant, unexpected, well-meaning question about her husband momentarily popped Maria out of her denial system. As she had with me, Maria had insinuated to everyone for thirty years that her husband was still alive. She had never donated or removed her husband's clothing or personal effects, which protected her from the deep misery and suffering of her loss.

In any case, if you suspect that unexpressed grief is the issue that's causing challenges with organizing, my suggestion is to join a grief and loss support group or speak to a qualified health practitioner. Allow yourself to grieve properly and completely, until you can breathe, eat, and sleep again in a natural pattern. If you want to declutter and get your home organized during periods of grieving, ask for help from caring friends and family members or hire a Clutter Remedy organizer. Anyone going through tough times can use the support and help of "friendly visitors" to help keep a home running when they are coping with the chaos of grief.

MENTAL HEALTH CHALLENGES

Some people have ongoing mental health challenges that will block them from getting organized and/or sabotage efforts to stay organized. When this happens I recommend seeking qualified health professionals to work with while using the Clutter Remedy strategy. While people with these challenges can still achieve perpetual organization, it's easier when they recognize their particular challenges and strategize solutions that help resolve those issues.

The more common mental health challenges that get in the way of organizing include OCD (obsessive-compulsive disorder), OCPD (obsessive-compulsive personality disorder), ADD (attention deficit disorder), ADHD (attention deficit hyperactivity disorder), and clinical depression. Of course, any other mental health challenge can also make it difficult to follow through on this process, including personality disorders, anxiety, brain injuries, PTSD, dementia, and addiction.

However, I'd like to share what I've learned about how people with certain mental health challenges manage their environments and tend to react to the organizing process. These aren't ways to diagnose an illness, nor are they ways to treat one, but they illustrate some of the particular issues that come up in relation to the Clutter Remedy strategy.

OCD symptoms revolve around cleaning fastidiously on the surface, but not seeing "the big picture" or the fine details of organizing. Rhia scrubbed her bathtub so hard with abrasives that she took off the enamel. A regular routine for Rhia was to focus on germs and wiping down the kitchen and bathroom countertops and all surfaces of her house three to four times daily. She was always complaining that her family "makes a mess," but oddly enough, her belongings were shoved into cabinets, on the floor of her closet, all over the laundry room, and piled in corners, and they were haphazardly getting trampled and tripped over. Meanwhile, Russ was an entrepreneur who spent close to four hours a day vacuuming his business's office space. In the bathroom, he put the toilet seat up and down, then back up and down, sometimes for hours, to make sure there was no bacteria. He called me for help to organize papers that had piled up for years in preparation for an audit. Russ hadn't paid taxes in nine years. Both Rhia and Russ entered treatment for their health challenges and were able to use the Clutter Remedy strategy successfully. Rhia reported, "Having a place for everything and willing myself to put things away has significantly reduced my stress." Russ relayed that he uses "categorizing and fine-tuning to keep up with his papers regularly."

OCPD, or obsessive-compulsive personality disorder, is completely different from OCD. Brian had an inability to release worn-out and useless items and became highly agitated when his wife, Mandy, and their kids touched his personal objects. When they wanted to get his things out of their way, he would say they were "ruining them." He worked night and day at his failing business, overthinking every project he had. Brian had an inability to focus and finish anything on time. His overly strict standards and rigidness of how things were to be done led to fatigue, hopelessness, and decreased motivation. Mandy set up guidelines and boundaries, and Brian agreed that not being there, during the process of categorizing and setting up the home, would be in everyone's best interest. When he came home after the organizing was completed and he was shown how we stored all his worldly goods, he was quite surprised by the idea of categorizing and fine-tuning, and agreed it was a better way to live. He also agreed to seek a qualified health professional for counseling to get to the root of his personality challenges.

ADD and ADHD can make it difficult to pay attention to detail and stay focused and follow through with finishing projects. Miranda had dreams and goals the size of New York, and she enjoyed talking about all she wanted to do in life and with her home, but accomplishing even the most simple task was difficult from start to finish. She lost things, couldn't stay on task, and was easily distracted. She explained that taking medication helped her get organized for a day or two, but "staying organized is tremendously difficult." One minute she would be emptying the dishwasher, and the next minute she would notice her dog and realize a walk would be beneficial for both of them. Miranda would not remember how she went from emptying the dishwasher to walking the dog. These shifts seemed to happen too fast.

Miranda described starting her day with an abundance of ideas for decluttering. She would rapidly empty everything she owned from her cabinets, closets, and cupboards. Without a plan, though, she would end up in the midst of piles and piles of stuff all over the place, unsure what to do and unable to make decisions. Then frustration and boredom would set in, and she would call a friend or find herself running out to shop for storage stuff she already owned. Miranda would have fourteen different projects going on at once and would take months to complete a few, if any. When I work with people with attention challenges, I help them understand what they value and how to change their language to become more decisive. With gentle guidance and redirection, Miranda was able to get every part of her home organized, with complete satisfaction, and to keep it that way. An objective third party is always useful when you are blocked by inattention and hyperactivity. Miranda called a few months later to tell me that what helps her stay organized the most is not only the Clear and Concise Criteria, but eliminating impeding language.

Depression, on the other hand, causes fatigue and severely decreased motivation. Depression combined with fatigue affects housework, paying bills, socializing, and physical functioning. Things tend to pile up and get completely out of sorts. Even getting out of bed can seem impossible, and people with depression will sleep day and night. Lack of energy or the inability to maintain energy for an extended period is a frequent issue.

Robin suffered from long-term depression, despite taking antidepressants, which kept her isolated and without a lot of friends or support. Then she lost both her parents within a short period of time. After they died, Robin had enough energy to get her parent's home cleared out and up for sale. Eventually, she faced her own mess in her tumultuous home and was able to get through her garage and kitchen before a huge bout of depression knocked her down again. For three years, Robin contacted me every autumn, and we would organize her home, but it was like starting over each time. In between each organizing session, Robin would collect more things, many of which she already owned. She couldn't maintain whatever we had done the year before, and her place became overflowing with new clutter. Robin explained that the reason she kept buying things she already had was because she didn't have the energy to search for what she wanted in her huge, tangly mess.

When I help people who suffer from depression get decluttered and categorized, I suggest that they have ongoing maintenance and support to help them put things away on a regular
basis throughout the year. When they wait for things to pile up,
it becomes overwhelming for them, and clutter takes over. Robin
eventually took my advice, and the last time I heard from her, she
said that regular maintenance was a "life changer."

YOU'RE AN EVER-CHANGING BEING
WITH AN EVER-CHANGING SPACE

You're always changing, every single second of your life, and your
space is always changing as well. Part of that reflects the cycles
and patterns of life, like seasonal changes, and part of that is the
flow and momentum of your goals and desires. You will always
seek to better yourself and identify how your values change to
achieve your ideal life. Self-discovery is a never-ending journey.

Achieving perpetual organization means, first, clarifying
your values and ideal life, and then clearing and organizing your
space to support that life. Who you are is, in many ways, reflected
by the stuff you keep: the memorabilia, collections, photos, books,
furniture, clothing, knickknacks, tools, sporting goods, artwork,
and all your worldly goods. So taking care of your things is part
of how you take care of yourself; your useful, treasured belongings deserve care and appreciation. In order to realize one's ideal
life, the temple of Apollo at Delphi instructed "Know thyself."
I agree, and I'd add "Know thy stuff" as well. This is what the
Clutter Remedy strategy provides.

Organization is not a one-time occurrence, because life is
constantly moving. Surprises come up all the time. Life never
stands still, and neither do you. Lives change, goals change, and
stuff changes, too. This means that, while you are not going to
be managing your stuff around the clock, perpetual organization

takes maintenance: a regular routine of review, self-reflection, adjustment, and revision as you fluctuate from more organized to less organized states. I encourage you to continually seek to know yourself, your space, and your stuff to understand and realize what still supports your ideal life. Then realign to restore the organized state that you achieved, and reinvent your space regularly so it is always organized in the way that best suits you.

The focus on maintaining order and following through to achieve it is the opposite of being a "human in a hamster wheel." Instead of the experience of being in constant motion, going round and round while getting nowhere, maintaining your organized masterpiece will be immensely satisfying. It will be a blissful experience of progression. Developing an ongoing organized lifestyle is about evolving to stay in sync with your life goals. The more you experience staying organized, the easier it becomes to grasp the many surprising benefits of a clutter-free life.

Everything that you own deserves a home where it gets to live permanently and to be with like items. Stuff matters, and matter does matter! When you take care of the objects you own, whether in your home or office, it is a reflection of how you treat yourself and others. Love yourself, love what you buy, love what you keep, and honor what you love and cherish by treating yourself and your things in a respectful, responsible manner.

ACKNOWLEDGMENTS

I want to thank my always-optimistic literary agent, Hilary Claggett, for believing that this project was world worthy and for signing me to her boutique literary agency, the Rudy Agency, and to the owner, Maryann Karinch, for all her encouragement. Hilary and Maryann, I appreciate you so much for all your hard work, trudging my book idea around, and finally getting it a wonderful home with New World Library. I want to thank Georgia Hughes for assisting me in the editing process and motivating me along the way. A big thank-you to Munro Magruder and Monique Muhlenkamp for their marketing prowess and determination and to all the New World Library people who helped publish this book, including Kristen Cashman, an extremely talented and easy-to-work-with editor who helped with the last stages.

A very special consideration to Raundi Moore-Kondo, my writing coach, for her passion and calming demeanor. A big shout-out and thank-you to all of you who helped me organize the book from the beginning: Brett Muiter, Rachel Messaros, Byron "Bear" Lansford, Shimona Hirchberg, Jane Friedman, Leslie Arambula, and Jeff Campbell. Thank you to all my big supporters: Lourdes Bennington, Corinne Haig, Nancy Daniel, Judy Masset, Lorraine Scott, Melissa Ehlert Traub, Michelle Rappaport, Mary Carlton, Jim Haboush, Janine Kubba, Byungim Park, and Karen Wacker. My heart is filled with gratitude for everyone who listened and lent a helping ear and hand.

ABOUT THE
AUTHOR

Marla Stone, MSW, is the owner of I-Deal-Lifestyle Inc., which provides decluttering, design, corporate training, and lifestyle coaching services. Before founding her company, Marla studied psychology and social work, and worked as a psychiatric social worker and psychotherapist. Throughout her career, Marla has sought to help her clients get to the root of their mental, emotional, spiritual, and environmental challenges. She has worked with military personnel and their families at Camp Pendleton on issues including PTSD, schizophrenia, bipolar disorder, OCD, depression, and personality challenges. She currently works with individuals and corporations on organization at all levels. She speaks at professional conferences and has an active following on social media. Her approach combines psychology, feng shui, design, and organizational skills. Learn more and connect to Marla by visiting her website, www.i-deal-lifestyle.com.

Praise for *The Clutter Remedy*

"Time is life's most valuable commodity, and in these busy days, who has time to organize? Marla Stone's book, *The Clutter Remedy*, provided the tools to succeed in organizing my business and personal life. This is the ultimate road map to stay organized for good and to live a more balanced life. Understanding what I truly value about life has freed me up to do what I enjoy and to know what to keep in my life. I made use of the enlightening tips to free my mind of stress and expand the bliss in my life."

— **Joseph Bennington**, CPA,
CFO of Habitat for Humanity of Orange County

"For me, the benefits of *The Clutter Remedy* have been immeasurable. With a clear, concise, supportive, and loving teaching style, Marla Stone helps to eliminate old habits of thought, emotion, and behavior, allowing positive new habits to emerge. Marla helps to remove blocks and barriers that interfere with your moving forward. What was unthinkable is now possible; what couldn't be seen is now visible and actionable."

— **Evelyn Gray**, productivity and stress-management coach
and consultant

"The path to a perpetually organized future passes through us, rather than around us. *The Clutter Remedy* is a strategy that addresses all aspects of the human experience: living and inanimate, past and future, wants and needs, dreams and desires. Marla's approach encourages the reader to live more, not just to have less. Starting today."

— **Lee Shuer**, coauthor of *The Buried in Treasures Workshop Facilitator's Guide*, creator of WRAP® for Reducing Clutter,
and recovering finder/keeper

"The Clutter Remedy strategies have helped my clients and me stay organized and neat for good. From my overall life to my teacups to my bags and shoes, my world has straightened up. The 'no get rid of' policy was my favorite part — no push to get rid of anything, but rather a wholesome philosophy and way to keep everything I love in order. I went from mini-overcollector to organized in days! The help Marla Stone has given my clients has made the sale of their homes quick and painless, and her packing strategy is the best I've ever seen."

— **Jeana Keough**, original cast member of *The Real Housewives of Orange County*, Coldwell Banker Realtor, and actress